SLAVE SONGS
OF THE
UNITED STATES

EDITED BY

William Francis Allen
Charles Pickard Ware
Lucy McKim Garrison

PREFACE BY
Harold Courlander

DOVER PUBLICATIONS, INC.
NEW YORK

Bibliographical Note

This Dover edition, first published in 1995, is an unabridged republication of the work originally published by A. Simpson & Co., New York, 1867. The Dover edition adds: a new preface written specially by Harold Courlander; a heading for the Introduction, p. i; and a part-title page for section IV (in the original edition, page 89 is followed by page 93). A few details of pitch and rhythm have been clarified in the music.

Library of Congress Cataloging-in-Publication Data

Slave songs of the United States / edited by William Francis Allen, Charles
  Pickard Ware, Lucky McKim Garrison ; preface by Harold Courlander.
    1 score.
    Originally published: New York : A. Simpson, 1867. With new preface.
    ISBN-13: 978-0-486-28573-3 (pbk.)
    ISBN-10: 0-486-28573-1 (pbk.)
    1. Afro-Americans—Music. 2. Folk music—United States. 3. Folk
  songs, English—United States. 4. Spirituals (Songs)—United States.
  5. Slaves—United States—Songs and music. I. Allen, William Francis,
  1830–1889. II. Ware, Charles Pickard, 1840–1921. III. Garrison, Lucy
  McKim, 1842–1877.
  M1670.S62   1995   95-7386
                                                                         CIP
                                                                          M

Manufactured in the United States by LSC Communications
28573112   2018
www.doverpublications.com

PREFACE TO THE DOVER EDITION.

The publication of *Slave Songs of the United States* in 1867 was, in its own way, something like our first orbital lunar flight. It was not the end but a beginning that helped set a course from which, thereafter, there would be no turning back. It brought us an awareness that African-American (then "negro") music constituted a genre different in many respects from other traditional American music—for example, that which had survived or developed within the English-speaking mainstream or the Louisiana French-Creole-Cajun population of Louisiana.

Not only was this music different, it was splendidly so, and far indeed from being "quaint" or "primitive," as it was sometimes described by inattentive observers. Nevertheless, many who were exposed to it in the earlier days of the nineteenth century were transfixed and charmed by what they heard of spirituals (sometimes called anthems), even though their understanding of the genre was not profound. Just what was it exactly? Hybrid African survivals or merely inventive copyings of the spirituals that were sung in white churches? Were the musical talents of "negro" people genetic? Many asserted so, though we now know that this music was a cultural, creative development that drew, as with all cultures, on various traditions.

The notations in the book, and of course the words, were set down mouth-to-ear by hand, the only way then known. Allen, Ware and Garrison put down what they heard or seemed to hear, usually trying to fit the rhythms into our established measures, frequently ignoring those purposive (not accidental) tones that were higher or lower than our usual scales allowed. In their earnest efforts to get everything down "right," they often had a singer repeat a song, only to find that a second singing was a little different. It was the beginning of an understanding that the tradition allowed the singer to perform a piece a little differently if he so wished. The small improvisations here and there might even enhance group singing. Melodies, as well as timing, were not set in stone.

I myself encountered the problem of mouth-to-ear transcribing of traditional music (as well as words) when I first worked with Haitian traditions three quarters of a century later. In second and third singings of a particular song, I observed that notes, words, timing and sometimes general structurings changed here and there. This is normal and commonplace in unwritten music. A few years later, recording equipment became available and simplified, as well as explained, everything.

Some of the pieces in *Slave Songs of the United States* did not come directly from mouth-to-ear, however. They might have been memorized by one enthusiast and resung to another. The authors were aware of, and apologized for, possible inaccuracies during the process. They need not have done so, however, for the overall collection opened the gates for a long line of investigators who followed over a period of more than a century, producing an abundant treasury of what this writer, at least, regards as probably the largest and richest single body of so-called "folk music" in the United States.

While some of our pioneers made their mark by geographical explorations of distant territories, the authors of *Slave Songs* made their explorations into much-neglected cultural material right at home. I cannot remember any serious writing on what we now call African-American traditional music that does not include *Slave Songs* in its bibliography.

HAROLD COURLANDER*

---

*A well-known novelist, folklorist, journalist and specialist on African and African-American cultures, Harold Courlander is the author of *Negro Folk Music, U.S.A.*, Dover, 1992 (0-486-27350-4).

SLAVE SONGS

OF THE

UNITED STATES.

New York:

A. SIMPSON & CO.,

1867.

[Original title page]

INTRODUCTION.

THE musical capacity of the negro race has been recognized for so many years that it is hard to explain why no systematic effort has hitherto been made to collect and preserve their melodies. More than thirty years ago those plantation songs made their appearance which were so extraordinarily popular for a while ; and if "Coal-black Rose," "Zip Coon" and "Ole Virginny nebber tire" have been succeeded by spurious imitations, manufactured to suit the somewhat sentimental taste of our community, the fact that these were called "negro melodies" was itself a tribute to the musical genius of the race. *

The public had well-nigh forgotten these genuine slave songs, and with them the creative power from which they sprung, when a fresh interest was excited through the educational mission to the Port Royal islands, in 1861. The agents of this mission were not long in dis-

---

* It is not generally known that the beautiful air "Long time ago," or "Near the lake where drooped the willow," was borrowed from the negroes, by whom it was sung to words beginning, "Way down in Raccoon Hollow."

covering the rich vein of music that existed in these half-barbarous people, and when visitors from the North were on the islands, there was nothing that seemed better worth their while than to see a "shout" or hear the "people" sing their "sperichils." A few of these last, of special merit,* soon became established favorites among the whites, and hardly a Sunday passed at the church on St. Helena without "Gabriel's Trumpet," "I hear from Heaven to-day," or "Jehovah Hallelujah." The last time I myself heard these was at the Fourth of July celebration, at the church, in 1864. All of them were sung, and then the glorious shout, "I can't stay behind, my Lord," was struck up, and sung by the entire multitude with a zest and spirit, a swaying of the bodies and nodding of the heads and lighting of the countenances and rhythmical movement of the hands, which I think no one present will ever forget.

Attention was, I believe, first publicly directed to these songs in a letter from Miss McKim, of Philadelphia, to *Dwight's Journal of Music*, Nov. 8, 1862, from which some extracts will presently be given. At about the same time, Miss McKim arranged and published two of them, "Roll, Jordan" (No. 1) and "Poor Rosy" (No. 8) —probably on all accounts the two best specimens that could be selected. Mr. H. G. Spaulding not long after gave some well-chosen specimens of the music in an article entitled "Under the Palmetto," in the *Continental*

---

* The first seven spirituals in this collection, which were regularly sung at the church.

Monthly for August, 1863, among them, "O Lord, re-member me" (No. 15), and "The Lonesome Valley" (No. 7). Many other persons interested themselves in the collection of words and tunes, and it seems time at last that the partial collections in the possession of the editors, and known by them to be in the possession of others, should not be forgotten and lost, but that these relics of a state of society which has passed away should be preserved while it is still possible.*

The greater part of the music here presented has been taken down by the editors from the lips of the colored people themselves; when we have obtained it from other sources, we have given credit in the table of contents. The largest and most accurate single collection in exist-ence is probably that made by Mr. Charles P. Ware, chiefly at Coffin's Point, St. Helena Island. We have thought it best to give this collection in its entirety, as the basis of the present work; it includes all the hymns as far as No. 43. Those which follow, as far as No. 55, were collected by myself on the Capt. John Fripp and neighboring plantations, on the same island. In all cases we have added words from other sources and other localities, when they could be obtained, as well as varia-tions of the tunes wherever they were of sufficient im-portance to warrant it. Of the other hymns and songs

---

* Only this last spring a valuable collection of songs made at Richmond, Va., was lost in the *Wagner*. No copy had been made from the original manuscript, so that the labor of their collection was lost. We had hoped to have the use of them in preparing the present work.

we have given the locality whenever it could be ascertained.

The difficulty experienced in attaining absolute correctness is greater than might be supposed by those who have never tried the experiment, and we are far from claiming that we have made no mistakes. I have never felt quite sure of my notation without a fresh comparison with the singing, and have then often found that I had made some errors. I feel confident, however, that there are no mistakes of importance. What may appear to some to be an incorrect rendering, is very likely to be a variation; for these variations are endless, and very entertaining and instructive.

Neither should any one be repelled by any difficulty in adapting the words to the tunes. The negroes keep exquisite time in singing, and do not suffer themselves to be daunted by any obstacle in the words. The most obstinate Scripture phrases or snatches from hymns they will force to do duty with any tune they please, and will dash heroically through a trochaic tune at the head of a column of iambs with wonderful skill. We have in all cases arranged one set of words carefully to each melody; for the rest, one must make them fit the best he can, as the negroes themselves do.

The best that we can do, however, with paper and types, or even with voices, will convey but a faint shadow of the original. The voices of the colored people have a peculiar quality that nothing can imitate; and the intonations and delicate variations of even one singer cannot be reproduced on paper. And I despair of conveying any notion of the effect of a number singing together, especially in a complicated shout, like "I can't stay behind, my Lord" (No. 8), or "Turn, sinner, turn O !" (No. 48). There is no singing in *parts*,* as we understand it, and yet no two appear to be singing the same thing—the leading singer starts the words of each verse, often improvising, and the others, who "base" him, as it is called, strike in with the refrain, or even join in the solo, when the words are familiar. When the "base" begins, the leader often stops, leaving the rest of his words to be guessed at, or it may be they are taken up by one of the other singers. And the "basers" themselves seem to follow their own whims, beginning when they please and leaving off when they please, striking an octave above or below (in case they have pitched the tune too low or too high), or hitting some other note that chords, so as to produce the effect of a marvellous complication and variety, and yet with the most perfect time, and rarely with any discord. And what makes it all the harder to unravel a thread of melody out of this strange network is that, like birds, they seem not infrequently to strike sounds that cannot be precisely represented by the gamut, and abound in

---

* "The high voices, all in unison, and the admirable time and true accent with which their responses are made, always make me wish that some great musical composer could hear these semi-savage performances. With a very little skilful adaptation and instrumentation, I think one or two barbaric chants and choruses might be evoked from them that would make the fortune of an opera."—*Mrs. Kemble's* "*Life on a Georgian Plantation,*" *p.* 218.

"slides from one note to another, and turns and cadences
not in articulated notes." "It is difficult," writes Miss
McKim, "to express the entire character of these negro
ballads by mere musical notes and signs. The odd turns
made in the throat, and the curious rhythmic effect pro·
duced by single voices chiming in at different irregular
intervals, seem almost as impossible to place on the
score as the singing of birds or the tones of an Æolian
Harp." There are also apparent irregularities in the
time, which it is no less difficult to express accurately,
and of which Nos. 10, 130, 131, and (eminently) 128, are
examples.

Still, the chief part of the negro music is *civilized* in
its character—partly composed under the influence of
association with the whites, partly actually imitated
from their music. In the main it appears to be original
in the best sense of the word, and the more we examine
the subject, the more genuine it appears to us to be. In
a very few songs, as Nos. 19, 23, and 25, strains of familiar
tunes are readily traced; and it may easily be that others
contain strains of less familiar music, which the slaves
heard their masters sing or play.*

On the other hand there are very few which are of an
intrinsically barbaric character, and where this character
does appear, it is chiefly in short passages, intermingled

---

* We have rejected as spurious "Give me Jesus," "Climb Jacob's Ladder,"
(both sung at Port Royal), and "I'll take the wings of the morning," which
we find in Methodist hymn-books. A few others, the character of which
seemed somewhat suspicious, we have not felt at liberty to reject without direct
evidence

with others of a different character. Such passages may
be found perhaps in Nos. 10, 12, and 18; and " Becky
Lawton," for instance (No. 29), "Shall I die?" (No. 52)
" Round the corn, Sally" (No. 87), and " O'er the
crossing" (No. 93) may very well be purely African in
origin. Indeed, it is very likely that if we had found it
possible to get at more of their secular music, we should
have come to another conclusion as to the proportion ot
the barbaric element. A gentleman in Delaware writes:

" We must look among their non-religious songs for
the purest specimens of negro minstrelsy. It is remarkable that they have themselves transferred the best or
these to the uses of their churches—I suppose on Mi.
Wesley's principle that 'it is not right the Devil should
have all the good tunes.' Their leaders and preachers
have not found this change difficult to effect; or at least
they have taken so little pains about it that one often
detects the profane *cropping out*, and revealing the origin of their most solemn ' hymns,' in spite of the best in-
tentions of the poet and artist. Some of the best *pure
negro* songs I have ever heard were those that used to
be sung by the black stevedores, or perhaps the crews
themselves, of the West India vessels, loading and un-
loading at the wharves in Philadelphia and Baltimore.
I have stood for more than an hour, often, listening to
them, as they hoisted and lowered the hogsheads and
boxes of their cargoes; one man taking the burden of
the song (and the slack of the rope) and the others
striking in with the chorus. They would sing in this

way more than a dozen different songs in an hour; most
of which might indeed be warranted to contain 'nothing
religious'—a few of them, 'on the contrary, quite the
reverse'—but generally rather innocent and proper in
their language, and strangely attractive in their music;
and with a volume of voice that reached a square or two
away. That plan of labor has now passed away, in Philadelphia at least, and the songs, I suppose, with it. So
that these performances are to be heard only among
black sailors on their vessels, or 'long-shore men in out-
of-the-way places, where opportunities for respectable
persons to hear them are rather few."

These are the songs that are still heard upon the Mississippi steamboats—wild and strangely fascinating—
one of which we have been so fortunate as to secure for
this collection. This, too, is no doubt the music of the
colored firemen of Savannah, graphically described by
Mr. Kane O'Donnel, in a letter to the Philadelphia
Press, and one of which he was able to contribute for our
use. Mr. E. S. Philbrick was struck with the resemblance of some of the rowing tunes at Port-Royal to the
boatmen's songs he had heard upon the Nile.

The greater number of the songs which have come into
our possession seem to be the natural and original pro-
duction of a race of remarkable musical capacity and
very teachable, which has been long enough associated
with the more cultivated race to have become imbued
with the mode and spirit of European music—often,
nevertheless, retaining a distinct tinge of their native
Africa.

The words are, of course, in a large measure taken from Scripture, and from the hymns heard at church; and for this reason these religious songs do not by any means illustrate the full extent of the debasement of the dialect. Such expressions as "Cross Jordan," "O Lord, remember me," "I'm going home," "There's room enough in Heaven for you," we find abundantly in Methodist hymn-books; but with much searching I have been able to find hardly a trace of the tunes. The words of the fine hymn, "Praise, member" (No. 5), are found, with very little variation, in "Choral Hymns" (No. 138). The editor of this collection informs us, however, that many of his songs were learned from negroes in Philadelphia, and Lt.-Col. Trowbridge tells us that he heard this hymn, before the war, among the colored people of Brooklyn.* For some very comical specimens of the way in which half-understood words and phrases are distorted by them, see Nos. 22, 23. Another illustration is given by Col. Higginson :†

"The popular camp-song of 'Marching Along' was entirely new to them until our quartermaster taught it to them at my request. The words 'Gird on the armor' were to·them a stumbling-block, and no wonder, until

---

* We have generally preserved the words as sung, even where clearly nonsensical, as in No. 89 ; so "Why don't you move so slow ?" (No. 22). We will add that "Paul and Silas, bound in jail" (No. 4), is often sung "Bounden Cyrus born in jail," and the words of No. 11 would appear as "I take my tex in Matchew and by de Revolutions—I know you by your gammon," &c.; so "Ringy Rosy Land" for "Ring Jerusalem."

† *Atlantic Monthly*, June, 1867.

some ingenious ear substituted 'Guide on de army,' which was at once accepted and became universal. 'We'll guide on de army, and be marching along,' is now the established version on the Sea Islands."

I never fairly heard a secular song among the Port Royal freedmen, and never saw a musical instrument among them. The last violin, owned by a "worldly man," disappeared from Coffin's Point "de year gun shoot at Bay Pint."* In other parts of the South, "fiddle-sings," "devil-songs," "corn-songs," "jig-tunes," and what not, are common; all the world knows the banjo, and the "Jim Crow" songs of thirty years ago. We have succeeded in obtaining only a very few songs of this character. Our intercourse with the colored people has been chiefly through the work of the Freedmen's Commission, which deals with the serious and earnest side of the negro character. It is often, indeed, no easy matter to persuade them to sing their old songs, even as a curiosity, such is the sense of dignity that has come with freedom. It is earnestly to be desired that some person, who has the opportunity, should make a collection of these now, before it is too late.

In making the present collection, we have only gleaned upon the surface, and in a very narrow field. The wealth of material still awaiting the collector can be guessed from a glance at the localities of those we have, and from

---

* i. e., November, 1861, when Hilton Head was taken by Admiral Dupont— a great date on the islands.

the fact, mentioned above, that of the first forty-three of the collection most were sung upon a single plantation, and that it is very certain that the stores of this plantation were by no means exhausted. Of course there was constant intercourse between neighboring plantations; also between different States, by the sale of slaves from one to another. But it is surprising how little this seems to have affected local songs, which are different even upon adjoining plantations. The favorite of them all, "Roll, Jordan" (No. 1), is sung in Florida, but not, I believe, in North Carolina. "Gabriel's Trumpet" (No. 4) and "Wrestle on, Jacob" (No 6) probably came from Virginia, where they are sung without much variation from the form usual at Port Royal; No. 6 is also sung in Maryland.* "John, John of the Holy Order" (No. 22) is traced in Georgia and North Carolina, and "O'er the Crossing" (No. 93) appears to be the Virginia original, variations of which are found in South Carolina, Georgia, and Tennessee. As illustrations of the slowness with which these songs travel, it may be mentioned that the "Graveyard" (No. 21), which was frequently sung on Capt. John Fripp's plantation in the winter of 1863–4, did not reach Coffin's Point (five miles distant) until the following Spring. I heard it myself at Pine Grove, two miles from the latter place, in March. Somewhere

---

* It is worthy of notice that a song much resembling "Poor Rosy" was heard last Spring from the boat hands of an Ohio River steamboat—the only words caught being "Poor Molly, poor gal."

upon this journey this tune was strikingly altered, as will be seen from the variation given, which is the form in which I was accustomed to hear it. Nos. 38, 41, 42, 43, 118, 119, 122, 123, were brought to Coffin's Point after Mr. Ware left, by refugees returning to the plantation from "town" and the Main. No. 74, likewise, "Nobody knows the trouble I see," which was common in Charleston in 1865, has since been carried to Coffin's Point, very little altered.

These hymns will be found peculiarly interesting in illustrating the feelings, opinions and habits of the slaves. Of the dialect I shall presently speak at some length. One of their customs, often alluded to in the songs (as in No. 19), is that of wandering through the woods and swamps, when under religious excitement, like the ancient bacchantes. To get religion is with them to "fin' dat ting." Molsy described thus her sister's experience in searching for religion: "Couldn't fin' dat leetle ting—hunt for 'em—huntin' for 'em all de time—las' foun' 'em." And one day, on our way to see a "shout," we asked Bristol whether he was going:—"No, ma'am, wouldn't let me in—hain't foun' dat ting yet—hain't been on my knees in de swamp." Of technical religious expressions, "seeker," "believer," "member," &c., the songs are full.

The most peculiar and interesting of their customs is the "shout," an excellent description of which we are permitted to copy from the N. Y. *Nation* of May 30, 1867:

"This is a ceremony which the white clergymen are inclined to discountenance, and even of the colored elders

some of the more discreet try sometimes to put on a face
of discouragement; and although, if pressed for Biblical warrant for the shout, they generally seem to think
'he in de Book,' or 'he dere-da in Matchew,' still it is
not considered blasphemous or improper if 'de chillen'
and 'dem young gal' carry it on in the evening for amuse-
ment's sake, and with no well-defined intention of 'praise.'
But the true 'shout' takes place on Sundays or on
'praise'-nights through the week, and either in the
praise-house or in some cabin in which a regular religious
meeting has been held. Very likely more than half the
population of the plantation is gathered together. Let it
be the evening, and a light-wood fire burns red before
the door of the house and on the hearth. For some
time one can hear, though at a good distance, the voci-
ferous exhortation or prayer of the presiding elder or of
the brother who has a gift that way, and who is not 'on
the back seat,'—a phrase, the interpretation of which is,
'under the censure of the church authorities for bad
behavior;'—and at regular intervals one hears the elder
'deaconing' a hymn-book hymn, which is sung two lines
at a time, and whose wailing cadences, borne on the
night air, are indescribably melancholy. But the
benches are pushed back to the wall when the formal
meeting is over, and old and young, men and women,
sprucely-dressed young men, grotesquely half-clad field-
hands—the women generally with gay handkerchiefs
twisted about their heads and with short skirts—boys
with tattered shirts and men's trousers, young girls bare-

footed, all stand up in the middle of the floor, and
when the 'sperichil' is struck up, begin first walking
and by-and-by shuffling round, one after the other, in a
ring. The foot is hardly taken from the floor, and the
progression is mainly due to a jerking, hitching motion,
which agitates the entire shouter, and soon brings out
streams of perspiration. Sometimes they dance silently,
sometimes as they shuffle they sing the chorus of the spiritual, and sometimes the song itself is also sung by the
dancers. But more frequently a band, composed or
some of the best singers and of tired shouters, stand at
the side of the room to 'base' the others, singing the
body of the song and clapping their hands together or
on the knees. Song and dance are alike extremely ener-
getic, and often, when the shout lasts into the middle of
the night, the monotonous thud, thud of the feet pre-
vents sleep within half a mile of the praise-house."

In the form here described, the "shout" is probably
confined to South Carolina and the States south of it. It
appears to be found in Florida, but not in North Carolina or Virginia. It is, however, an interesting fact that
the term "shouting" is used in Virginia in reference to
a peculiar motion of the body not wholly unlike the
Carolina shouting. It is not unlikely that this remarkable religious ceremony is a relic of some native African
dance, as the Romaika is of the classical Pyrrhic.
Dancing in the usual way is regarded with great horror
by the people of Port Royal, but they enter with infinite
zest into the movements of the "shout." It has its

connoisseurs, too. "Jimmy great shouter," I was told; and Jimmy himself remarked to me, as he looked patronizingly on a ring of young people, "Dese yere worry deyseff—we don't worry weseff." And indeed, although the perspiration streamed copiously down his shiny face, he shuffled round the circle with great ease and grace.

The shouting may be to any tune, and perhaps all the Port Royal hymns here given are occasionally used for this purpose; so that our cook's classification into "sperichils" and "runnin' sperichils" (shouts), or the designation of certain ones as sung "just sittin' round, you know," will hardly hold in strictness. In practice, however, a distinction is generally observed. The first seven, for instance, favorite hymns in the St. Helena church, would rarely, if ever, be used for shouting; while probably on each plantation there is a special set in common use. On my plantation I oftenest heard "Pray all de member" (No. 47), "Bell da ring" (No. 46), "Shall I die?" (No. 52), and "I can't stay behind, my Lord" (No. 8). The shouting step varied with the tune; one could hardly dance with the same spirit to "Turn, sinner," or "My body rock 'long fever," as to "Rock o' Jubilee," or "O Jerusalem, early in de morning." So far as I can learn, the shouting is confined to the Baptists; and it is, no doubt, to the overwhelming preponderance of this denomination on the Sea Islands that we owe the peculiar richness and originality of the music there

The same songs are used for rowing as for shouting. I know only one pure boat-song, the fine lyric, "Michael row the boat ashore" (No. 31); and this I have no doubt is a real spiritual—it being the archangel Michael that is addressed. Among the most common rowing tunes were Nos. 5, 14, 17, 27, 28, 29, 30, 31, 32, 33, 36, 46. "As I have written these tunes," says Mr. Ware, "two measures are to be sung to each stroke, the first measure being accented by the beginning of the stroke, the second by the rattle of the oars in the rowlocks. On the passenger boat at the [Beaufort] ferry, they rowed from sixteen to thirty strokes a minute; twenty-four was the average. Of the tunes I have heard, I should say that the most lively were 'Heaven bell a-ring' (No. 27), 'Jine 'em' (No. 28), 'Rain fall' (No. 29), 'No man' (No. 14), 'Bell da ring' (No. 46), and 'Can't stay behind;' and that 'Lay this body down' (No. 26), 'Religion so sweet' (No. 17), and 'Michael row' (No. 31), were used when the load was heavy or the tide was against us. I think that the long hold on 'Oh,' in 'Rain fall,' was only used in rowing. When used as a 'shout' I am quite sure that it occupied only one measure, as in the last part of the verse. One noticeable thing about their boat-songs was that they seemed often to be sung just a trifle behind time; in 'Rain fall,' for instance, 'Believer cry holy' would seem to occupy more than its share of the stroke, the 'holy' being prolonged till the very beginning of the next stroke; indeed, I think Jerry often hung on his oar a little just there before dipping it again."*

As to the composition of these songs, "I always won-dered," says Col. Higginson, "whether they had always a conscious and definite origin in some leading mind, or whether they grew by gradual accretion, in an almost unconscious way. On this point I could get no infor-mation, though I asked many questions, until at last, one day when I was being rowed across from Beaufort to Ladies' Island, I found myself, with delight, on the ac-tual trail of a song. One of the oarsmen, a brisk young fellow, not a soldier, on being asked for his theory of the matter, dropped out a coy confession. 'Some good sperituals,' he said, 'are start jess out o' curiosity. I been a-raise a sing, myself, once.'

"My dream was fulfilled, and I had traced out, not the poem alone, but the poet. I implored him to pro-ceed.

"'Once we boys,' he said, 'went for tote some rice, and de nigger-driver, he keep a-callin' on us; and I say, 'O, de ole nigger-driver!' Den anudder said, 'Fust ting my mammy told me was, notin' so bad as nigger-drivers.' Den I made a sing, just puttin' a word, and den anudder word.'

"Then he began singing, and the men, after listening a moment, joined in the chorus as if it were an old ac-

---

* For another curious circumstance in rowing, see note to "Rain fall," No. 29.

quaintance, though they evidently had never heard it before. I saw how easily a new 'sing' took root among them."

A not inconsistent explanation is that given on page 12 of an "Address delivered by J. Miller McKim, in Sansom Hall, Philadelphia, July 9, 1862."

"I asked one of these blacks—one of the most intelligent of them [Prince Rivers, Sergeant 1st Reg. S. C. V.] —where they got these songs. 'Dey make 'em, sah.' 'How do they make them?' After a pause, evidently casting about for an explanation, he said : 'I'll tell you, it's dis way. My master call me up, and order me a short peck of corn and a hundred lash. My friends see it, and is sorry for me. When dey come to de praise-meeting dat night dey sing about it. Some's very good singers and know how ; and dey work it in—work it in, you know, till they get it right; and dat's de way.' A very satisfactory explanation ; at least so it seemed to me."

We were not so fortunate as Col. Higginson in our search for a poet. Cuffee at Pine Grove did, to be sure, confess himself the author of " Climb Jacob's Ladder ;"— unfortunately, we afterwards found it in a Northern hymn book. And if you try to trace out a new song, and ask, "Where did you hear that?" the answer will be, "One strange man come from Eding's las' praise-night and sing 'em in praise-house, and de people catch 'em;" or "Titty 'Mitta [sister Amaritta] fetch 'em from Polawana, where she tuk her walk gone spend Sunday. Some of her fahmly sing 'em yonder." "But what does

'Ringy rosy land' [Ring Jerusalem, No. 21] mean ?"
"Me dunno."

Our title, "Slave Songs," was selected because it best described the contents of the book. A few of those here given (Nos. 64, 59) were, to be sure, composed since the proclamation of emancipation, but even these were inspired by slavery. "All, indeed, are valuable as an expression of the character and life of the race which is playing such a conspicuous part in our history. The wild, sad strains tell, as the sufferers themselves could, of crushed hopes, keen sorrow, and a dull, daily misery, which covered them as hopelessly as the fog from the rice swamps. On the other hand, the words breathe a trusting faith in rest for the future—in ' Canaan's air and happy land,' to which their eyes seem constantly turned."

Our original plan hardly contemplated more than the publication of the Port Royal spirituals, some sixty in all, which we had supposed we could obtain, with perhaps a few others in an appendix. As new materials came into our hands, we enlarged our plan to the present dimensions. Next to South Carolina, we have the largest number from Virginia; from the other States comparatively few. Few as they are, however, they appear to indicate a very distinct character in different States. Contrary to what might be expected, the songs from Virginia are the most wild and strange. " O'er the Crossing" (No. 93) is peculiarly so; but "Sabbath has no end" (No. 89), "Hypocrite and Concubine" (No. 91),

"O shout away" (No. 92), and "Let God's saints come in" (No. 99), are all distinguished by odd intervals and a frequent use of chromatics. The songs from North Carolina are also very peculiar, although in a different way, and make one wish for more specimens from that region. Those from Tennessee and Florida are most like the music of the whites.

We had hoped to obtain enough secular songs to make a division by themselves; there are, however, so few of these that it has been decided to intersperse them with the spirituals under their respective States. They are highly characteristic, and will be found not the least interesting of the contents of this work.

It is, we repeat, already becoming difficult to obtain these songs. Even the "spirituals" are going out of use on the plantations, superseded by the new style of religious music, " closely imitated from the white people, which is solemn, dull and nasal, consisting in repeating two lines of a hymn and then singing it, and then two more, *ad infinitum*. They use for this sort of worship that one everlasting melody, which may be remembered by all persons familiar with Western and Southern camp-meetings, as applying equally well to long, short or common metre. This style of proceeding they evidently consider the more dignified style of the two, as being a closer imitation of white, genteel worship—having in it about as little soul as most stereotyped religious forms of well instructed congregations."*

---

* Mrs. H. B. Stowe, in *Watchman and Reflector*, April, 1867.

It remains to speak of points connected with the ty-pography of the songs.

We have aimed to give all the characteristic variations which have come into our hands, whether as single notes or whole lines, or even longer passages; and of words as well as tunes. Many of these will be found very in-teresting and instructive. The variations in words are given as foot-notes—the word or group of words in the note, to be generally substituted for that which precedes the mark: and it may be observed, although it seems hardly necessary, that these variations are endless; such words as "member," "believer," "seeker," and all names, male and female, may be brought in wherever appropriate. We have not always given all the sets of words that we have received often they are improvised to such an extent that this would be almost imprac-ticable. In Nos. 16, 17, 19, etc., we have given them very copiously, for illustration; in others we have omit-ted the least interesting ones. In spelling, we proposed to ourselves the rule well stated by Col. Higginson at the commencement of his collection: "The words will be here given, as nearly as possible, in the original dia-lect; and if the spelling seems sometimes inconsistent, or the misspelling insufficient, it is because I could get no nearer."

As the negroes have no part-singing, we have thought it best to print only the melody; what appears in some places as harmony is really variations in single notes. And, in general, a succession of such notes turned in the same direction indicates a single longer variation. Words in a parenthesis, with small notes, (as "Brudder Sammy" in No. 21), are interjaculatory; it has not, however, been possible to maintain entire consistency in this matter. Sometimes, as "no man" and "O no man," in No. 14, interchangeable forms are put, for convenience sake, in different parts of the tune.

It may sometimes be a little difficult, for instance in Nos. 9, 10, 20 and 27, to determine precisely which part of the tune each verse belongs to ; in these cases we have endeavored to indicate it as clearly as is in our power. However much latitude the reader may take in all such matters, he will hardly take more than the negroes themselves do.   In repeating, it may be observed that the custom at Port Royal is to repeat the first part of the tune over and over, it may be a dozen times, before passing to the "turn," and then to do the same with that.   In the Virginia songs, on the other hand, the chorus is usually sung twice after each verse—often the second time with some such interjaculatory expression as "I say now," "God say you must," as given in No. 99.

We had some thought of indicating with each the *tempo* of the different songs, but have concluded to print special directions for singing by themselves.   It should be remarked, however, that the same tune varied in quickness on different occasions.   "As the same songs," writes Miss McKim, "are sung at every sort of work, of course the *tempo* is not always alike.   On the water, the oars dip 'Poor Rosy' to an even *andante;* a stout boy and girl at the hominy mill will make the same 'Poor Rosy' fly, to keep up with the whirling stone; and in the evening, after the day's work is done, 'Heab'n shall-a be my home' peals up slowly and mournfully from the distant quarters. One woman, a respectable house-servant, who had lost all but one of her twenty-two children, said to me : 'Pshaw ! don't har to dese yer chil'en, missee. Dey just rattles it off—dey don't know how for sing it. I likes 'Poor Rosy' better dan all de songs, but it can't be sung widout *a full heart and a troubled sperrit.*

The rests, by the way, do not indicate a cessation in the music, but only in part of the singers. They over-lap in singing, as already described, in such a degree that at no time is there any complete pause. In "A House in Paradise" (No. 40) this overlapping is most marked.

It will be noticed that we have spoken chiefly of the negroes of the Port Royal islands, where most ot our observations were made, and most of our materials col-lected. The remarks upon the dialect which follow have reference solely to these islands, and indeed almost exclu-sively to a few plantations at the northern end of St. Hel-ena Island. They will, no doubt, apply in a greater or less degree to the entire region of the southeasterly slave States, but not to other portions of the South. It should also be understood that the corruptions and peculiarities here described are not universal, even here. There are

all grades, from the rudest field-hands to mechanics and
house-servants, who speak with a considerable degree of
correctness, and perhaps few would be found so illiterate
as to be guilty of them all.

Ordinary negro talk, such as we find in books, has
very little resemblance to that of the negroes of Port
Royal, who have been so isolated heretofore that they
have almost formed a dialect of their own.   Indeed, the
different plantations have their own peculiarities, and
adepts profess to be able to determine by the speech of
a negro what part of an island he belongs to, or even, in
some cases, his plantation.   I can myself vouch for the
marked peculiarities of speech of one plantation from
which I had scholars, and which was hardly more than
a mile distant from another which lacked these peculiarities.   Songs, too, and, I suppose, customs, vary in the
same way.

A stranger, upon first hearing these people talk, especially if there is a group of them in animated conversa-
tion, can hardly understand them better than if they
spoke a foreign language, and might, indeed, easily
suppose this to be the case.   The strange words and
pronunciations, and frequent abbreviations, disguise the
familiar features of one's native tongue, while the rhythmical modulations, so characteristic of certain European languages, give it an utterly un-English sound.
After six months' residence among them, there were
scholars in my school, among the most constant in at-
tendance, whom I could not understand at all, unless
they happened to speak very slowly.

With these people the process of "phonetic decay" appears to have gone as far, perhaps, as is possible, and with it an extreme simplification of etymology and syntax. There is, of course, the usual softening of *th* and *v*, or *f*, into *d* and *b*; likewise a frequent interchange of *v* and *w*, as *veeds* and *vell* for *weeds* and *well*; *woices* and *punkin wine*, for *voices* and *pumpkin vine*. "De wile' (*vilest*) sinner may return" (No. 48). This last example illustrates also their constant habit of clipping words and syllables, as *lee' bro',* for *little brother; plänt'shun,* for *plantation.* The lengthening of short vowels is illustrated in both these (*a*, for instance, rarely has its short English sound). "Een (in) dat mornin' all day" (No. 56).

Strange words are less numerous in their *patois* than one would suppose, and, few as they are, most of them may be readily derived from English words. Besides the familiar *buckra*, and a few proper names, as Cuffy, Quash, and perhaps Cudjo, I only know of *churray* (spill), which may be "throw 'way;" *oona* or *ona*, "you" (both singular and plural, and used only for friends), as "Ona build a house in Paradise" (No. 40) ; and *aw*, a kind of expletive, equivalent to "to be sure," as, "Dat clot' cheap." "Cheap aw." "Dat Monday one lazy boy." "Lazy aw—I 'bleege to lick 'em."

Corruptions are more abundant. The most common of them are these: *Yearde* (hear), as in Nos. 3, etc. "Flora, did you see that cat?" "No ma'am, but I yearde him holler." "*Sh'um*," a corruption of *see 'em*, applied (as *'em* is) to all genders and both numbers.

"Wan' to see how Beefut (Beaufort) stan'—nebber sh'um since my name Adam." *Huddy* (how-do?), pronounced *how-dy* by purists, is the common term of greeting, as in the song No. 20, "Tell my Jesus huddy O." " Bro' (brother) Quash sen' heap o' howdy." *Studdy*, (steady) is used to denote any continued or customary action. "He studdy 'buse an' cuss we," was the complaint entered by some little children against a large girl. " I studdy talk hard, but you no yearde me," was Rina's defence when I reproved her for not speaking loud enough. When we left, we were told that we must " studdy come back." Here, however, it seems to mean *steady*. *Titty* is used for mother or oldest sister; thus, Titty Ann was the name by which the children of our man-of-all work knew their mother, Ann. *Sic-a* or *sake-a*, possibly a condensation of *same* and *like*. " Him an' me grow up sic-a brudder an' sister." *Enty* is a curious corruption, I suppose of *ain't he*, used like our " Is that so ? " in reply to a statement that surprises one. " Robert, you have n't written that very well." " Enty, sir? " John, it's going to rain to-day." " Enty, sir?" *Day-clean* is used for *day-break*. " Do, day-clean, for let me go see Miss Ha'yet ; and de day wouldn't clean." *Sun-up* is also common. *Chu'* for "this" or "that there;" as " Wha' chu ? " "See one knife chu ? " *Say* is used very often, especially in singing, as a kind of expletive; " (Say) when you get to heaven (say) you 'member me." (No. 27.) "Ain't you know say cotton de-de ?" In the last sentence " de-de " (accent on first syllable) means

" is there ;"—the first *de*, a corruption of *does* for *is*, will be explained presently ; the other is a very common form for *dere*, there.

I do not remember any other peculiar words, but several words used peculiarly. *Cuss* is used with great latitude, to denote any offensive language. " Him cuss me 'git out." " Ahvy (Abby) do cuss me," was the serious-sounding, but trifling accusation made by a little girl against her seat-mate. *Stan'* is a very common word, in the sense of *look*. " My back stan' like white man," was a boast which meant that it was not scarred with the lash. " Him stan' splendid, ma'am," of the sitting of a dress. I asked a group of boys one day the color of the sky. Nobody could tell me. Presently the father of one of them came by, and I told him their ignorance, repeating my question with the same re- sult as before. He grinned : " Tom, how sky stan'? " " Blue," promptly shouted Tom. *Both* they seldom use ; generally " all-two," or emphatically, " all-two boff to- gedder." *One* for *alone*. " Me one, and God," answered an old man in Charleston to the question whether he es- caped alone from his plantation. " Gone home one in de dark," for alone. " Heab'n 'nuff for me one " (*i.e.*, I suppose, "for my part "), says one of their songs (No. 46.) *Talk* is one of their most common words, where we should use *speak* or *mean*. "Talk me, sir?" asks a boy who is not sure whether you mean him or his comrade. "Talk lick, sir? nuffin but lick," was the answer when I asked whether a particular master used to

whip his slaves. *Call* is used to express relationship;
as, "he call him aunt." *Draw*, for receiving in any
way — derived from the usage of drawing a speci-
fic amount of supplies at stated times. "Dey draw
letter," was the remark when a mail arrived and
was distributed among us whites. *Meet* is used in the
sense of *find*. " I meet him here an' he remain wid me,"
was the cook's explanation when a missing chair was
found in the kitchen. When I remarked upon the
absurdity of some agricultural process—" I meet 'em so,
an' my fader meet 'em so," was the sufficient answer. A
grown man, laboring over the mysteries of simple addition, explained the gigantic answer he had got by " I
meet two row, and I set down two." "I meet you dere,
sir," said Miller frankly, when convinced in an argument.
Too *much* is the common adverb for a high degree of a
quality; "he bad *too* much " was the description of a hard
master. *Gang*, for any large number ; " a whole gang of
slate-pencils." *Mash* in the sense of crush ; " mammy
mash 'em," when the goat had killed one of her kids by
lying on it. *Sensibble* and *hab sense* are favorite expressions. A scholar would ask me to make him " sensibble"
of a thing. " Nebber sh'um since I hab sense" (*i.e.*, since
I was old enough to know). *Stantion* (substantial) was
a favorite adjective at Coffin's Point. *Strain* is also a
favorite word. " Dem boy strain me," explained Billy,
when some younger boys were attempting to *base* him.
" I don't want to give more nor fifty-five dollar for a
horse," said Quash, " but if dey strain you, you may
give fifty-six." " Dat tune *so* strainful," said Rose.

The letters *n*, *r* and *y* are used euphonically. " He de baddes' little gal from y'ere to n'Europe," said Bristol of his troublesome niece Venus; " ought to put him on a bar'l, an' den he fall 'sleep an' fall down an' hut heself, an' dat make him more sensibble." " He n'a comin', sir," was often said of a missing scholar. At first I took the *n* for a negative. I set Gib one day to picking out *E's* from a box of letters. He could not distinguish *E* from *F*, and at last, discouraged with his repeated failures, explained, holding out an *F*, " dis y'ere stan' sic-a-r-*um*." (This looks like that.) It is suggested also that *d* is used in the same way, in " He d'a comin';" and *s*, in singing, for instance, " 'Tis wells and good" (No. 25). So the vowel *a*; " De foxes have-a hole" (No. 2), "Heaven bell a-ring" (No. 27).

The most curious of all their linguistic peculiarities is perhaps the following. It is well known that the negroes in all parts of the South speak of their elders as " uncle" and " aunt,—"* from a feeling of politeness, I do not doubt; it seemed disrespectful to use the bare name, and from *Mr.* and *Mrs.* they were debarred. On the Sea Islands a similar feeling has led to the use of *cousin* towards their equals. Abbreviating this, after their fashion, they get *co'n* or *co'* (the vowel sound *u* as in *cousin*) as the common title when they speak of one another; as, C'Abram, Co' Robin, Co'n Emma, C'Isaac, Co'Bob. *Bro'* (brother) and *Si'* (sister) and even *T'* (Tit-

---

* In South Carolina " daddy" and "maum " are more common.

ty) are also often used in the same way; as, Bro' Paris,
Si' Rachel, T' Jane.   A friend insists that *Cudjo* is
nothing but Co' Joe.

Where and *when* are hardly used, at least by the
common class of negroes.   The question " Where did
you spill the milk ? " was answered only with a stare ;
but " which way milk churray ? " brought a ready re-
sponse.   " What side you stayin', sir ? " was one of the
first questions put to me.   Luckily I had been initiated,
and was able to answer it correctly.

There is probably no speech that has less inflection,
or indeed less power of expressing grammatical relation
in any way.   It is perhaps not too strong to say that the
field-hands make no distinction of gender, case, number,
tense, or voice.   The pronouns are to be sure distinguished more or less by the more intelligent among
them, and all of these, unless perhaps *us*, are occasionally heard.   *She* is rare; *her* still more so; *him* being
commonly used for the third person singular of all cases
and genders; *'em*, if my memory serves me rightly, only
for the objective case, but for all genders and both numbers.   *He*, or *'e*, is, I should think, most common as
possessive.   " Him lick we " might mean a girl as well
as a boy.   Thus *we* is distinguished from *I* or *me*, and
dey or *dem* from *him* or *dat ;* and these are, I think, the
only distinctions made in number.   " Dat cow," is singular, " dem cow" plural; " Sandy hat" would mean in-
differently Sandy's hat or hats ; " nigger-house " means
the collection of negro-houses, and is, I suppose, really a
plural.

I do not know that I ever heard a real possessive case, but they have begun to develop one of their own, which is a very curious illustration of the way inflectional forms grow up. If they wish to make the fact of possession at all emphatic or distinct, they use the word "own." Thus, they will say "Mosey house," but if asked whose house that is, the answer is "Mosey own." "Co' Molsy y'own" was the odd reply made by Mylie to the question whose child she was carrying. Literally translated, this is "Molsy's;" *Co'* is title, *y* euphonic. An officer of a colored regiment standing by me when the answer was made—himself born a slave—confessed that it was mere gibberish to him. No doubt this custom would in time develop a regular inflectional possessive ; but the establishment of schools will soon root up all these original growths.

Very commonly, in verbs which have strong conjugations, the forms of the past tense are used for the present; "What make you leff we?" "I tuk dem brudder" (No. 30). Past time is expressed by *been*, and less commonly *done*. "I been kep him home two day," was the explanation given for a daughter's absence from school. "I done pit my crap in de groun'." Present time is made definite by the auxiliary *do* or *da*, as in the refrains "Bell da ring," "Jericho da worry me." (Nos. 46, 47). "Bubber (brother) da hoe he tater." So *did* occasionally : "Nat did cuss me," complained one boy of another. It is too much to say that the verbs have no inflections, but it is true that these have nearly disappeared.　Ask a boy where he is going, and the answer is "gwine crick for ketch crab" (going into the creek to catch crabs); ask another where the missing boy is, and the answer is the same, with *gone* instead of *gwine*. The hopeless confusion between auxiliaries is sometimes very entertaining : as "de-de," "ain't you know?" "I didn't been." "De Lord is perwide" (No. 2). "You'd better pray, de worl' da [is] gwine" (No. 14). "My stomach been-a da hut me."

Some of these sentences illustrate two other peculiarities—the omission of auxiliaries and other small words, and the use of *for* as the sign of the infinitive. "Unky Taff call Co' Flora for drop tater." "Good for hold comb" was the wisest answer found to the teacher's question what their ears were good for. "Co' Benah wan' Mr.— for tuk 'em down," was Gib's whispered comment when the stubborn Venus refused to step down from a bench. After school the two were discovered at fisticuffs, and on being called to account—"dat same Benah dah knock me," said Gib, while Venus retorted with "Gib cuss me in school."

It is owing to this habit of dropping auxiliaries that the passive is rarely if ever indicated. You ask a man's name, and are answered, "Ole man call John." "Him mix wid him own fät," was the description given of a paste made of bruised ground-nuts, the oil of the nut furnishing moisture. "I can't certain," "The door didn't fasten," "The bag won't full," "Dey frighten in de dark," are illustrations of every-day usage.

Proper names furnish many curious illustrations of the corruption in pronunciation. Many of them are impossible to explain, and it is still only a surmise that *Finnick* is derived from *Phœnix*, and *Wyna* from *Malvina* (the first syllable being dropped, as in *'Nelius* for *Cornelius*, and *'Rullus* for *Marullus*.) *Hacless* is unquestionably *Hercules*, and *Sack* no doubt *Psyche*; *Strappan* is supposed to be *Strephon*. All these are common names on the Sea Islands. Names of trades, as *Miller*, *Butcher*, are not uncommon. One name that I heard of, but did not myself meet with, was *After-dark*, so called because he was so black that " you can't sh'um 'fo' dayclean."

In conclusion, some actual specimens of talk, illustrating the various points spoken of, may not be without interest. A scene at the opening of school:*

" Charles, why did n't you come to school earlier?" " A-could n't come *soon* to-day, sir; de boss he sheer out clo' dis mornin'." " What did he give you?" " Me, sir? I ain't *git;* de boss he de baddest buckra ebber a-see. De morest part ob de mens dey git heaps o' clo'—more'n 'nuff; 'n I ain't git nuffin." " Were any other children there?" " Plenty chil'n, sir. All de chil'n dah fo' sunup." " January, you have n't brought your book." " I *is*, sir; sh'um here, sir?" " Where is Juno?" " I ain't

---

* It is proper to state that most of the materials for this scene were furnished by Mr. Arthur Sumner, which accounts for the similarity of certain of the expressions to those in the dialogue given in the September number of the Boston *Freedman's Record.*

know where he gone, sir." "Where is Sam?" "He
didn't been here." "Where is the little boy, John?"
"He pick up he foot and run." A new scholar is
brought: "Good mornin', maussa; I bring dis same chile
to school, sir: *do* don't let 'em stay arter school done.
Here you, gal, stan' up an' say howdy to de genlmn. Do
maussa lash 'em well ef he don't larn he lesson." "Where's
your book, Tom?" "Dunno, sir. Some*body* mus' a tief
'em." "Where's your brother?" "Sh'um dar? wid
bof he han' in he pocket?" "Billy, have you done your
sum?" "Yes, sir, I out 'em." "Where's Polly?"
"Polly de-de." Taffy comes up. "Please, sir, make me
sensibble of dat word—I want to ketch 'em werry bad,
sir, werry bad." Hacless begins to read. He spells
in a loud whisper, "g-o; g-o; g-o—can't fetch dat word,
sir, nohow."

The first day Gib appeared in school I asked him
whether he could read, and received a prompt answer in
the affirmative. So, turning to the first page of Willson's
Primer, I told him to read. The sentence was "I am
on," or something of that sort, opposite a picture of a
boy on a rocking-horse. Gib attacked it with great
volubility, "h-r-s-e, horse. De boy is on top ob de
horse"—adding some remarks about a chair in the
background. His eye then fell on a picture of an eagle,
and without pausing he went on, "De raben is big bird."
Next he passed to a lion on the opposite page, "D-o-g,
dog;" but just then a cut above, representing a man
and an ox, proved too strong for him, and he proceeded

to give a detailed history of the man and the cow. When this was completed, he took up a picture of a boy with a paper soldiers'-cap and a sword. "Dis man hab sword; he tuk' e sword an' cut' e troat." Here I checked him, and found, as may be expected, that he did not know a single letter.

A scene at a government auction: Henry and Titus are rivals, bidding for a piece of "secesh" furniture. Titus begins with six dollars. "Well, Titus, I won't strain you—eight." "Seven," says Titus. "Ten," says Henry. "Twelve," says Titus. "And den." said our informant, "Henry bid fourteen an' tuk 'em for fifteen."

One day when we returned from a row on the creek, to make a call, Dick met us with his face on a grin: "You seen him? you seen Miss T? *I* seen him. I tole him you gone wid intention call on she, but de boat didn't ready in time. He cotch you at Mr. H., on'y de horse bodder him at de gate." One of the boys came to me one day with the complaint, "Dem Ma' B. Fripp chil'n fin' one we book," *i. e.*, those children from Mr. T. B. Fripp's have found one of our books. "'E nebber crack 'e bret," *i. e.*, say a word. "What make you don't?" "Mr. P. didn't must." "I don't know what make I didn't answer." "How do you do to-day?" "Stirrin,"; "spared," "standin';" "out o' bed," (never "very well.") Or, of a friend, "He feel a lee better'n he been, ma'am."

"Arter we done chaw all de hard bones and swallow all de bitter pills," was part of a benediction; and the prayer at a "praise-meeting" asked "dat all de white bredren an' sister what jine praise wid we to-night might be bound up in de belly-band ob faith." At a funeral in a colored regiment: "One box o' dead meat gone to de grave to-day—who gwine to-morrow? Young man, who walk so stiff—ebery step he take seem like he say, 'Look out dah, groun', I da comin'." The following is Strappan's view of Love. " Arter you lub, you lub, you know, boss. You can't broke lub. Man can't broke lub. Lub stan'—'e ain't gwine broke. Man hab to be berry smart for broke lub. Lub is a ting stan' jus' like tar; arter he stick, he stick, he ain't gwine move. He can't move less dan you burn him. Hab to kill all two arter he lub 'fo' you broke lub."

It would be an interesting, and perhaps not very diffi-cult inquiry, to determine how far the peculiarities of speech of the South Carolina negroes result from the large Huguenot element in the settlement of that State. It would require, however, a more exact acquaintance than I possess with the dialects of other portions of the South, to form a judgment of any value upon this point. Meanwhile, I will say only that two usages have struck me as possibly arising from this source, the habitual length-ening of vowel sounds, and the pronunciation of *Maussa*, which may easily have been derived from *Monsieur*. After all, traces of Huguenot influence should by right be found among the whites, even more than the blacks.

[W. F. A.]

IT remains for the Editors to acknowledge the aid they have received in making this compilation. To Col. T. W. HIGGINSON, above all others, they are indebted for friendly encouragement and for direct and indirect contributions to their original stock of songs. From first to last he has manifested the kindest interest in their undertaking, constantly suggesting the names of persons likely to afford them information, and improving every opportunity to procure them material. As soon as his own valuable collection had appeared in the *Atlantic Monthly*, he freely made it over to them with a liberality which was promptly confirmed by his publishers, Messrs. TICKNOR & FIELDS. It is but little to say that without his co-operation this *Lyra Africana* would have lacked greatly of its present completeness and worth. Through him we have profited by the cheerful assistance of Mrs. CHARLES J. BOWEN, Lieut.-Colonel C. T. TROWBRIDGE, Capt. JAMES S. ROGERS, Rev. HORACE JAMES, Capt. GEO. S. BARTON, Miss LUCY GIBBONS, Mr. WILLIAM A. BAKER, Mr. T. E. RUGGLES, and Mr. JAMES SCHOULER. Our thanks are also due for contributions, of which we have availed ourselves, to Dr. WILLIAM A. HAMMOND, Mr. GEO. H. ALLAN, Lt.-Col. WM. LEE APTHORP, Mr. KANE O'DONNEL, Mr. E. J. SNOW, Miss CHARLOTTE L. FORTEN, Miss LAURA M. TOWNE, and Miss ELLEN MURRAY; and for criticisms, suggestions, communications, and unused but not unappreciated contributions, to Mr. JOHN R. DENNETT, Miss ANNIE MITCHELL, Mr. REUBEN TOMLINSON, Mr. ARTHUR SUMNER, Mr. N. C. DENNETT, Miss MARY ELLEN

PEIRCE, Maj.-Gen. WAGER SWAYNE, Miss MARIA W. BEN-
TON, Prof. J. SILSBY, Rev. JOHN L. MCKIM, Mr. ALBERT
GRIFFIN, Mr. A. S. JENKS, Mr. E. H. HAWKES, Rev. H. C.
TRUMBULL, Rev. J. K. HOSMER, Rev. F. N. KNAPP, Brev.
Maj.-Gen. TRUMAN SEYMOUR, Maj.-Gen. JAMES H. WIL-
SON, Mr. J. H. PALMER, and others; and, finally, to the
editors of various newspapers who gratuitously an-
nounced the forthcoming volume.

Conscious of many imperfections in this, the result of
not inconsiderable joint labor for nearly a year, the Editors submit it, nevertheless, to the public judgment, in
the belief that it will be pronounced deserving of even
greater pains and of permanent preservation.

WILLIAM FRANCIS ALLEN,
CHARLES PICKARD WARE,
LUCY MCKIM GARRISON.

CONTENTS.

PART II.

PART III.

PART IV.

DIRECTIONS FOR SINGING.

IN addition to those already given in the Introduction, the following explanations may be of assistance :

Where all the words are printed with the music, there will probably be little difficulty in reading the songs; but where there are other words printed below the music, it will often be a question to which part of the tune these words belong, and how the refrain and the chorus are to be brought in.

It will be noticed that the words of most of the songs arrange themselves into stanzas of four lines each. Of these some are *refrain*, and some are *verse* proper. The most common arrangement gives the second and fourth lines to the refrain, and the first and third to the verse; and in this case the third line may be a repetition of the first, or may have different words. Often, however, the refrain occupies only one line, the verse occupying the other three; while in one or two songs the verse is only one line, while the refrain is three lines in length. The refrain is repeated with each stanza : the words of the verse are changed at the pleasure of the leader, or fugleman, who sings either well-known words, or, if he is gifted that way, invents verses as the song goes on.

In addition to the stanza, some of the songs have a chorus, which usually consists of a fixed set of words, though in some of the songs the chorus is a good deal varied. The refrain of the main stanza often appears in the chorus. The stanza can always be distinguished from the chorus, in those songs which have more than one stanza, by the figure "1" placed before the stanza which is printed with the music; the verses below being numbered on "2," "3," "4," &c. In a few cases the first verse below the music is numbered "3 ;" this occurs when two verses have been printed above in the music, instead of the first verse being repeated. When the chorus has a variety of words, the additional verses are printed below without numbers.

In the following list the first fifty tunes in the collection are classified according to the peculiarity of their division into verse and refrain. It is hoped that this will help to remove all obscurities with which the reader may be embarrassed.

No explanation is needed for Nos. 2, 12, 13, 18, 22-26, 34, 36, 38-43.

Single line and refrain, 27, 35.

    "   "   " with chorus, 6, 29.

Stanza of 4 lines :

No refrain ; chorus, 11.

4th line refrain ; introduction, 7.

    "   " chorus, 8, 9, 10, 15, 37, 45.

1st and 2d lines verse, 3d and 4th refrain ; chorus, 1, 4.

1st and 3d   " " 2d and 4th refrain, 14, 17, 20, 28, 31, 32, 33, 47, 48, 49, 50.

1st and 3d lines verse, 2d and 4th refrain ; double, 21.

    "   "   "   "   " chorus, 3, 30, 44.

    "   "   "   •"   " introduction, 46.

1st line verse ; chorus, 5.

    "   " (double) ; chorus, 19.

3d   " " , 16.

As regards the *tempo*, most of the tunes are in 2-4 time, and in most of these $\musnote = 100$—(say) 100-120. The spirit of the music will determine the *tempo* within these limits. The slower tunes are 1, 3, 9, 17, 21, etc. No. 2 is about $\musnote = 160$-180, and perhaps had better have been written in 3-8. So No. 13 would be better in 2-4 ; as it is, the $\musnote = 160$-170. No. 24 should be read as if divided in 2-4, with $\musnote = 100$. The *tempo* of the rowing tunes has been already indicated.

The pitch has generally been accommodated to voices of medium range.

Slave Songs of the United States.

I.

SOUTH-EASTERN SLAVE STATES:

Including South Carolina, Georgia, and the Sea Islands.

SLAVE SONGS OF THE UNITED STATES.

I.

1. ROLL, JORDAN, ROLL.

1. My brudder* sit-tin' on de tree of life, An' he yearde when Jor-dan roll ; Roll, Jor-dan, Roll, Jor-dan, Roll, Jor-dan, roll ! O march de an - gel march, O march de an - gel march ; O my soul a - rise in Heaven, Lord, For to yearde when Jor-dan roll.

2 Little chil'en, learn to fear de Lord,
  And let your days be long;
  Roll, Jordan, &c.

3 O, let no false nor spiteful word
  Be found upon your tongue ;
  Roll, Jordan, &c.

* Parson Fuller, Deacon Henshaw, Brudder Mosey, Massa Linkum, &c.

[This spiritual probably extends from South Carolina to Florida, and is one of the best known and noblest of the songs.]

2

2. JEHOVAH, HALLELUJAH.

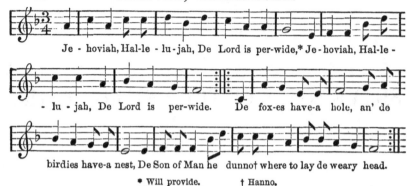

Je - hoviah, Hal-le - lu-jah, De Lord is per-wide,* Je-hoviah, Hal-le - lu - jah, De Lord is per-wide. De fox-es have-a hole, an' de birdies have-a nest, De Son of Man he dunnot where to lay de weary head.

* Will provide.   † Hanno.

1 HEAR FROM HEAVEN TO-DAY.

Hur - ry* on, my wea - ry soul, And I yearde from heaven to - day, Hur-ry on, my weary† soul, And I yearde from heaven to - day.

1. My sin is for - giv - en and my soul set free, And I yearde from heaven to - day, My sin is for - giv - en, and my soul set free, And I year - de from heav - en to - day.

2 A baby born in Bethlehem,
    And I yearde, &c.

3 De trumpet sound in de oder bright land.‡

4 My name is called and I must go.

5 De bell is a-ringin' in de oder bright world.

* Travel.   † My brudder, Brudder Jacob, Sister Mary.   ‡ World.

4. BLOW YOUR TRUMPET, GABRIEL.

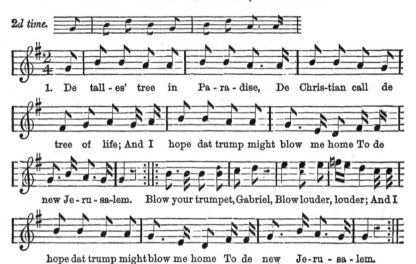

2d time.

1. De tall-es' tree in Pa-ra-dise, De Chris-tian call de tree of life; And I hope dat trump might blow me home To de new Je-ru-sa-lem. Blow your trumpet, Gabriel, Blow louder, louder; And I hope dat trump might blow me home To de new Je-ru-sa-lem.

2 Paul and Silas, bound in jail,
Sing God's praise both night and day;
And I hope, &c.

[This hymn is sung in Virginia in nearly the same form. The following minor variation is given by Mrs. Bowen, as heard by her in Charleston, some twenty-five years ago:]

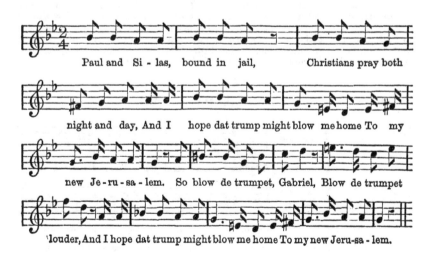

Paul and Si-las, bound in jail, Christians pray both night and day, And I hope dat trump might blow me home To my new Je-ru-sa-lem. So blow de trumpet, Gabriel, Blow de trumpet louder, And I hope dat trump might blow me home To my new Jeru-sa-lem.

4

5. **PRAISE, MEMBER.**

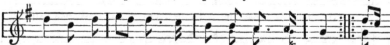

Praise, member,* praise God, I praise my Lord un - til I   die;

Praise, member, praise God, †And reach de heaven-ly   home. ‡ 1. O

Jor-dan's bank § is   a   good old   bank, And I   hain't but one more

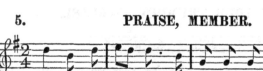

riv-er   to cross; I want some valiant sol-dier   To help me bear the cross.

    2 O soldier's fight is a good old fight,
       And I hain't, &c.

    3 O I look to de East, and I look to de West.

    4 O I wheel to de right, and I wheel to de left.

    * Believer.   † Religion so sweet.   ‡ Shore.   § Stream, Fight.

[The last verse is varied in several different ways; Col. Higginson gives, "There's a hill on my leff, an' he catch on my right," and says, "I could get no explanation of this last riddle, except, 'Dat mean, if you go on de leff, you go to 'struction, and if you go on de right, go to God, for sure.'" Miss Forten gives, "I hop on my right an' I catch on my leff," and supposes "that some peculiar motion of the body formed the original accompaniment of the song, but has now fallen into disuse." Lt. Col. Trowbridge heard this hymn sung among the colored people of Brooklyn, N. Y., several years ago.]

6. **WRESTLE ON, JACOB.**

1. I hold my brudder* wid a   tremblin' han', De Lord will

bless my soul. † Wrastl' on, Ja-cob, Ja-cob, day is a-breakin',

    * My sister, Brudder Jacky, All de member.   † I would not let him go.

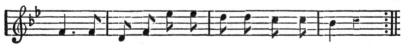

Wrastl' on, Ja - cob, Oh he* would not let him go.

2 I will not let you go, my Lord.
3 Fisherman Peter out at sea.
4 He cast † all night and he cast † all day.
5 He ‡ catch no fish, but he ‡ catch some soul.
6 Jacob hang from a tremblin' limb.

* Lord I.   † Fish.   ‡ L

[This is also sung in Maryland and Virginia, in a slightly modified form. A Virginia verse is, —

I looked to the East at the breaking of the day,
The old ship of Zion went sailing away.]

7.   THE LONESOME VALLEY.

My brudder, *want to get re-li-gion?   Go down in de lonesome valley, etc.

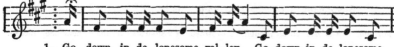

1. Go down in de lonesome val-ley, Go down in de lonesome

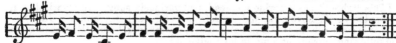

valley, my Lord; Go down in de lonesome valley, To meet my Je-sus dere.

2 O feed on milk and honey.
3 O John he write de letter.
4 And Mary and Marta read 'em.

* Sister Katy, etc.

["'De valley,' and ' de lonesome valley'. were familiar words in their religious experience. To descend into that region implied the same process with the 'anxious-seat' of the camp-meeting. When a young girl was supposed to enter it, she bound a handkerchief by a peculiar knot over her head, and made it a point of honor not to change a single garment till the day of her baptism, so that she was sure of being in physical readiness for the cleansing rite, whatever her spiritual mood might be. More than once, in noticing a damsel thus mystically kerchiefed, I have asked some dusky attendant its meaning, and have received the unfailing answer, - framed with their usual indifference to the genders of pronouns,—' He in de lonesome valley, sa.' "—*Col. Higginson.*]

8. I CAN'T STAY BEHIND.

Chor. I can't stay be-hind, my Lord, I can't stay be-hind!

1. Dere's room e-nough, Room e-nough, Room e-nough in de

heaven, my Lord;* Room enough, Room enough, I can't stay be-hind.

2 I been all around, I been all around,
Been all around de Heaven, my Lord.

3 I've searched every room—in de Heaven, my Lord. †

4 De angels singin' ‡—all round de trone.

5 My Fader call—and I must go.

6 Sto-back, § member; sto-back, member.

* **For you.** † And Heaven all around. ‡ Crowned. § "Sto-back" means "Shout backwards."

[This "shout" is very widely spread, and variously sung. In Charleston it is simpler in its movement, and the refrain is "I can't stay away." In Edgefield it is expostulating: "Don't stay away, my mudder." Col. Higginson gives the following version, as sung in his regiment:

"O, my mudder is gone! my mudder is gone!
My mudder is gone into heaven, my Lord!
        I can't stay behind!
Dere 's room in dar, room in dar.
Room in dar, in de heaven, my Lord!
        I can't stay behind.
Can't stay behind, my dear,
        I can't stay behind!

"O, my fader is gone! &c.

"O, de angels are gone! &c

"O, I 'se been on de road! I 'se been on de road!
I 'se been on de road into heaven, my Lord!
        I can't stay behind!
O, room in dar, room in dar,
Room in dar, in de heaven, my Lord!
        I can't stay behind!"

Lt. Col. Trowbridge is of opinion that it was brought from Florida, as he first heard it in Dec , 1862, from a boat-load of Florida soldiers brought up by Lt. Col. Billings. It was not heard by Mr. Ware at Coffin's Point until that winter. It seems hardly likely, however, that it could have made its way to Charleston and Edgefield since that time. The air became "immensely popular" in the regiment, and was soon adopted for military purposes, so that the class leaders indignantly complained of "the drum corps using de Lord's chune."]

9. POOR. ROSY.

1. Poor Ro - sy, poor gal;* Poor Ro - sy, poor gal;
Ro - sy break my poor heart, Heav'n shall-a be my home. I
can - not stay in hell one day, Heav'n shall-a be my home; I'll
sing and pray my soul a-way, Heav'n shall-a be my home.

2 Got hard trial in my way, (ter)
  Heav'n shall-a be my home.
  O when I talk,† I talk † wid God, } (bis)
  Heav'n shall-a be my home. }

3 I dunno what de people‡ want of me, (ter)
  Heav'n shall-a be my home.

* Poor Cæsar, poor boy.   † Walk.   ‡ Massa.

[This song ranks with "Roll, Jordan," in dignity and favor. The following variation of the second part was heard at "The Oaks:"]

Be - fore I stay in hell one day, Heaven shall-a be my home;
I sing and pray my soul a - way, Heaven shall-a be my home.

8

10. THE TROUBLE OF THE WORLD.

1. I want to be* my Fa-der's chil'-en, I want to be my Fa-der's chil'-en, I want to be my Fa-der chil'-en,

Roll, Jor-dan, roll. O say,†ain't you done wid de

trou-ble ob de world, Ah!.... trou-ble ob de world, Ah!

Say ain't you done wid de trou-ble ob de world, Ah Roll, Jor-dan, roll.

2 I ask de Lord how long I hold 'em, (*ter*)
  Hold 'em to de end.

3 My sins so heavy I can't get along, Ah! &c.

4 I cast my sins in de middle of de sea, Ah! &c.

* O you ought to be.   † My sister, My mudder, etc.

[This is perhaps as good a rendering of this strange song as can be given.
The difficulty is in the time, which is rapid, hurried and irregular to a degree
which is very hard to imitate and impossible to represent in notes. The following is sung in Savannah, with the same refrain, " Trouble of the world:"]

I wish I was in ju-bi-lee, Ha, ju-bi-lee; I

wish I was in ju-bi-lee, Roll, Jor-dan, roll.

11. THERE'S A MEETING HERE TO-NIGHT.

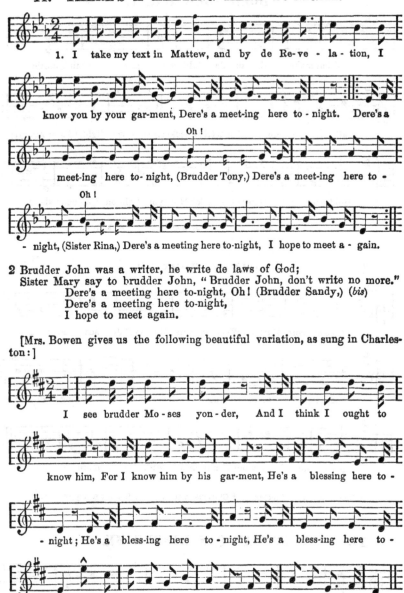

1. I take my text in Mattew, and by de Re-ve-la-tion, I know you by your gar-ment, Dere's a meet-ing here to-night. Dere's a meet-ing here to-night, (Brudder Tony,) Dere's a meet-ing here to-night, (Sister Rina,) Dere's a meeting here to-night, I hope to meet a-gain.

2 Brudder John was a writer, he write de laws of God;
Sister Mary say to brudder John, "Brudder John, don't write no more."
  Dere's a meeting here to-night, Oh! (Brudder Sandy,) (*bis*)
  Dere's a meeting here to-night,
  I hope to meet again.

[Mrs. Bowen gives us the following beautiful variation, as sung in Charleston:]

I see brudder Mo-ses yon-der, And I think I ought to know him, For I know him by his gar-ment, He's a blessing here to-night; He's a bless-ing here to-night, He's a bless-ing here to-night, And I think I ought to know him, He's a bless-ing here to-night.

12. ### HOLD YOUR LIGHT.

What make ole Sa-tan da fol-low me so? Sa-tan hain't nottin' at

all for to do wid* me. (Run seeker.) Hold your light, (Sister Ma-ry,†)

Hold your light, (Seeker turn back,) Hold your light on Ca-naan shore.

* Long o'. † All de member, Turn seeker.

13. ### HAPPY MORNING.

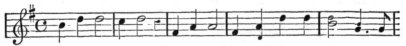

Weep no more, Marta, Weep no more, Ma ry,* Je-sus rise from de

dead, Hap-py† morn - ing. Glo-rious‡ morn - ing, Glo-rious

morn - ing, My Sa-viour rise from de dead, Happy morn - ing.

* Doubt no more, Thomas. † Glorious, Sunday. ‡ O what a happy Sunday.

14. ### NO MAN CAN HINDER ME.

Walk in, kind Sa - viour, No man can hin-der me! Walk in, sweet

Je - sus, No man can hin - der me! 2. See what won - der Je - sus done,

O no man can hin - der me! See what won - der Je - sus done,

O no man can hin-der me! O no man, no man, no man can

hin - der me! O no man, no man, no man can hin-der me!

3 Jesus make de dumb to speaĸ.

4 Jesus make de cripple walk.

5 Jesus give de blind his sight.

6 Jesus do most anyting.

7 Rise, poor Lajarush, from de tomb.

8 Satan ride an iron-gray horse.

9 King Jesus ride a milk-white horse.

Variation.

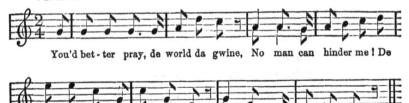

You'd bet - ter pray, de world da gwine, No man can hinder me! De

Lord have mer - cy on my soul, No man can hin - der me!

15. ## LORD, REMEMBER ME.

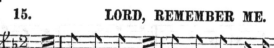

1. Oh Deat' he is a lit - tle man, And he goes from do' to

do', He kill some souls and he wound*d* some, And he lef' some souls to pray.

Oh* Lord, re - mem - ber me, Do, Lord, re - mem - ber me; Re -

- mem - ber me† as de year roll round, Lord, re - member me.

2 I want to die like-a Jesus die,
    And he die wid a free good will,
  I lay out in de grave and I stretchee out e arms,
    Do, Lord, remember me.

      * Do.   † I pray (cry) to de Lord.

16. ## NOT WEARY YET.

O me no wea- ry yet, O me no wea- ry yet 1. I

have a wit-ness in my heart, O me no weary yet. (Brudder Tony *)

2 Since I been in de field to † fight.

3 I have a heaven to maintain.

4 De bond of faith are on my soul.

5 Ole Satan toss a ball at me.

6 Him tink de ball would hit my soul.

7 De ball for hell and I for heaven.

    * Sister Mary.   † Been-a.

17. RELIGION SO SWEET.

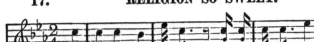

1. O walk Jor-dan long road, And re - li-gion so sweet; O re- li-gion is good for a - ny-ting, And re - li-gion so sweet.

3 Religion make you happy.*

4 Religion gib me patience.†

5 O member, get religion.

6 I long time been a-huntin'.

7 I seekin' for my fortune.

8 O I gwine to meet my Savior.

9 Gwine to tell him 'bout my trials.

10 Dey call me boastin' member.

11 Dey call me turnback‡ Christian.

12 Dey call me 'struction maker.

13 But I don't care what dey call me.

14 Lord, trial 'longs to a Christian.

15 O tell me 'bout religion.

16 I weep for Mary and Marta.

17 I seek my Lord and I find him

* Humble.   † Honor, Comfort.   ‡ Lyin', 'ceitful.

18. HUNTING FOR THE LORD.

Hunt till you find him, Halle - lu - jah, And a - huntin' for de

Lord; Till you find him, Halle - lu - jah, And a - huntin' for de Lord.

19. GO IN THE WILDERNESS.

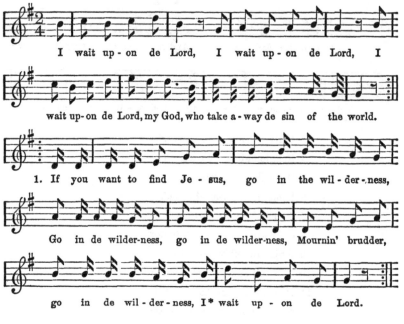

I wait up-on de Lord, I wait up-on de Lord, I wait up-on de Lord, my God, who take a-way de sin of the world.

1. If you want to find Je-sus, go in the wil-der-ness, Go in de wilder-ness, go in de wilder-ness, Mournin' brudder, go in de wil-der-ness, I* wait up-on de Lord.

3 You want to be a Christian.

4 You want to get religion.

5 If you spec' to be converted.

6 O weepin' Mary.

7 'Flicted sister.

8 Say, ain't you a member?

9 Half-done Christian.

10 Come, backslider.

11 Baptist member.

12 O seek, brudder Bristol.

13 Jesus a waitin' to meet you in de wilderness.

ro.

[The second part of this spiritual is the familiar Methodist hymn " Ain't I glad I got out of the wilderness! " and may be the original. The first part is very beautiful, and appears to be peculiar to the Sea Islands.]

20. TELL MY JESUS "MORNING."

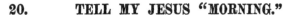

1. In de mornin' when I rise, Tell my Je-sus huddy, oh ;* I

wash my hands in de morn-in' glo-ry, Tell my Je-sus huddy, oh.

Variation to first line.

Pray To-ny, pray boy, you got de or-der;

2 Mornin', Hester, mornin', gal,
   Tell my Jesus, &c.

(To the Variation.)

2 Say, brudder Sammy, you got de order,
   Tell my Jesus, &c.

3 You got de order, and I got de order.

      ✦ Morning.

21. THE GRAVEYARD.

(Brudder Sammy) 1. Who gwine to lay dis bo-dy, Member, O, shout

glo-ry.* And-a who gwine to lay dis bo-dy, Oh ring Je-ru-sa-lem.

2. O call all de member to de graveyard. Mem-ber, &c.

3 O graveyard, ought to know me.

4 O grass grow in de graveyard.

5 O I reel† and I rock in de graveyard.

    ✦ Sing glory, Graveyard.   † Shout, Wheel.

6 O I walk and I toss wid Jesus.

7 My mudder reel and-a toss wid de fever.

8 I have a grandmudder in de graveyard.

9 O where d'ye tink I find 'em?*

10 I find 'em, Lord, in de graveyard.

11 (Member,) I wheel, and I rock, and I gwine home.

12 (Brudder Sammy) O 'peat dat story over.

Variation to Verse 3.

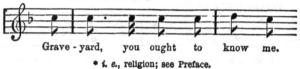

Grave - yard, you ought to know me.

* *i. e.,* religion; see Preface.

22. JOHN, JOHN, OF THE HOLY ORDER.

John, John, wid de ho - ly or - der,* Sit - tin' on de gol - den

or - der; John, John, wid de ho - ly or - der, Sit-tin' on de gol - den

or - der; John, John, wid de ho - ly or - der, Sit-tin' on de gol - den

or - der, To view de pro - mised land. O Lord, I weep, I

mourn, Why don't you move so slow? I'm a hunt - in' for some

guard - ian an - gel Gone a - long be - fore. Ma-ry and Mar-ta,

* John, John, de holy Baptist.

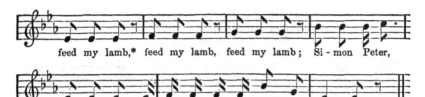

feed my lamb,* feed my lamb, feed my lamb; Si - mon Peter,

feed my lamb, a - sit - tin' on de gol - den or - der.

* Paul and Silas, bound in jail.

[These words were sung at Hilton Head to the second and third parts:

> I went down sing polka, and I ax him for my Saviour;
> I wonder de angel told me Jesus gone along before.
> I mourn, I pray, although you move so slow;
> I wonder, &c.

The regularity and elaborateness of this hymn lead one at first to suspect its genuineness. The question seems, however, to be settled by two very interesting and undoubted variations from North Carolina and Georgia. The following words were sung at Augusta, but we have not been able to obtain the tune, which is entirely unlike that given above. For the North Carolina variation, see No. 130. Both, as will be seen, omit the second part, and a comparison of the two shows that the enigmatical word "order" should undoubtedly be "altar." The North Carolina tune has the first part quite different from the Port Royal tune, the last very similiar to it.

> Oh John, John, de holy member,
> Sittin' on de golden ban'.
> O worldy, worldy, let him be,
> Let him be, let him be;
> Worldy, worldy, let him be,
> Sittin' on de golden ban'.]

23. I SAW THE BEAM IN MY SISTER'S EYE.

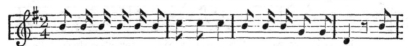

1. I saw de beam in my sister's * eye, Can't saw de beam in mine; You'd

bet - ter lef' your sis - ter door, Go keep your own door clean.

> 2 And I had a mighty battle like-a Jacob and de angel,
> Jacob, time of old;
> I didn't 'tend to lef' 'em go
> Till Jesus bless my soul.

* Titty Peggy, Brudder Mosey, &c.

3 And blessèd me, and blessèd my,
 And blessèd all my soul;
I didn't 'tend to lef' 'em go
 Till Jesus bless my soul.

[This tune appears to be borrowed from "And are ye sure the news is true?"—but it is so much changed, and the words are so characteristic, that it seemed undoubtedly best to reta n it.]

24. **HUNTING FOR A CITY.**

I am huntin' for a ci-ty, to stay a-while, I am huntin' for a ci-ty, to stay awhile, I am huntin' for a ci-ty, to stay a-while, O be-lie-ver got a home at las

25. **GWINE FOLLOW.**

Tit-ty Ma-ry, you know I gwine fol-low, I gwine fol-low, gwine fol-low, Brudder William, you know I gwine to fol-low, For to do my Fa-der will. 'Tis well and good I'm a-comin' here tonight, I'm a-com-in' here to-night, I'm a-com-in' here to-night, 'Tis well and good, I'm a-comin' here tonight, For to do my Fader will.

[The second part of this tune is evidently "Buffalo" (variously known also as "Charleston" or "Baltimore") "Gals;" the first part, however, is excellent and characteristic.]

26. LAY THIS BODY DOWN.

1. O grave - yard, O grave - yard, I'm
walk - in' troo de grave - yard; Lay dis bo - dy down.

2 *I know moonlight, I know starlight,
I'm walkin' troo de starlight;
Lay dis body down.

* O moonlight (*or* moonrise); O my soul, O your soul.

[This is probably the song heard by W. H. Russell, of the London *Times*, as described in chapter xviii. of "My Diary North and South." The writer was on his way from Pocotaligo to Mr. Trescot's estate on Barnwell Island, and of the midnight row thither he says:

"The oarsmen, as they bent to their task, beguiled the way by singing in unison a real negro melody, which was unlike the works of the Ethiopian Serenaders as anything in song could be unlike another. It was a barbaric sort of madrigal, in which one singer beginning was followed by the others in unison, repeating the refrain in chorus, and full of quaint expression and melancholy:—

    ' Oh your soul! oh my soul! I'm going to the churchyard
      To lay this body down;
    Oh my soul! oh your soul! we're going to the churchyard
      To lay this nigger down.'

And then some appeal to the difficulty of passing the 'Jawdam' constituted the whole of the song, which continued with unabated energy during the whole of the little voyage. To me it was a strange scene. The stream, dark as Lethe, flowing between the silent, houseless, rugged banks, lighted up near the landing by the fire in the woods, which reddened the sky—the wild strain, and the unearthly adjurations to the singers' souls, as though they were palpable, put me in mind of the fancied voyage across the Styx."

We append with some hesitation the following as a variation; the words of which we borrow from Col. Higginson. Lt. Col. Trowbridge says of it that it was sung at funerals in the night time—one of the most solemn and characteristic of the customs of the negroes. He attributes its origin to St. Simon's Island, Georgia:]

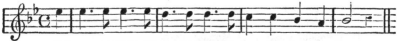

I know moonlight, I know starlight; I lay dis bo - dy down.

2 I walk in de moonlight, I walk in de starlight;
I lay dis body down.

3 I know de graveyard, I know de graveyard,
When I lay dis body down.

4 I walk in de graveyard, I walk troo de graveyard,
    To lay, &c.
5 I lay in de grave an' stretch out my arms ;
    I lay, &c.
6 I go to de judgment in de evenin' of de day
    When I lay, &c.
7 And my soul an' your soul will meet in de day
    When we lay, &c.

[" 'I'll lie in de grave and stretch out my arms.' Never, it seems to me, since man first lived and suffered, was his infinite longing for peace uttered more plaintively than in that line."—*Col. Higginson.*]

27.   HEAVEN BELL A-RING.

1. My Lord, my Lord, what shall I do ? And a heav'n bell a-ring and praise God.

Variation second.

Timmy, Timmy,   or - phan boy.   Robert, Robert,   or - phan child.

2 What shall I do for a hiding place ? And a heav'n, &c.
3 I run to de sea, but de sea run dry.
4 I run to de gate, but de gate shut fast.
5 No hiding place for sinner dere.
6 Say you when you get to heaven say you 'member me.
7 Remember me, poor fallen soul.*
8 Say when you get to heaven say your work shall prove.
9 Your righteous Lord shall prove 'em well.
10 Your righteous Lord shall find you out.
11 He cast out none dat come by faith.
12 You look to de Lord wid a tender heart.
13 I wonder where poor Monday dere.
14 For I am gone and sent to hell.
15 We must harkee what de worldy say.
16 Say Christmas come but once a year.
17 Say Sunday come but once a week.

        * When I am gone, For Jesus' sake.

28. **JINE 'EM.**

On Sunday mornin' I seek my Lord; Jine 'em, jine 'em oh! Oh jine 'em, be-lie-ver, jine 'em so; Jine 'em, jine 'em oh!

[For other words see "Heaven bell a-ring," No. 27. The following were sung at Hilton Head, probably to the same tune:

Join, brethren, join us O,
Join us, join us O.
We meet to-night to sing ana pray;
In Jesus' name we'll sing and pray.

A favorite rowing tune: apparently a variation of "Turn sinner," No. 48.]

29. **RAIN FALL AND WET BECCA LAWTON.**

Rain fall and wet * Becca Lawton,† Oh....... Rain fall and wet Bec-ca Law-ton, Oh! Brudder ‡ cry ho-ly!

1. Been § back ho-ly, I must come slow-ly; Oh! Brudder cry ho-ly!

2 Do, Becca Lawton, come to me yonder.

3 Say, brudder Tony, what shall I do now?

4 Beat back holy, and rock salvation.

* Sun come and dry. † All de member, &c. ‡ We all, Believer, &c. § Beat, Bent, Rack.

["Who," says Col. Higginson, "*Becky Martin* was, and why she should or should not be wet, and whether the dryness was a reward or a penalty, none could say. I got the impression that, in either case, the event was posthumous, and that there was some tradition of grass not growing over the grave of a sinner; but even this was vague, and all else vaguer."

Lt. Col. Trowbridge heard a story that "*Peggy Norton* was an old prophetess, who said that it would not do to be baptized except when it rained; if the Lord

was pleased with those who had been 'in the wilderness,' he would send rain."
Mr. Tomlinson says that the song always ends with a laugh, and appears therefore to be regarded by the negroes as mere nonsense. He adds that when it is
used as a rowing tune, at the words "Rack back holy!" one rower reaches over
back and slaps the man behind him, who in turn does the same, and so on.]

30.   BOUND TO GO.

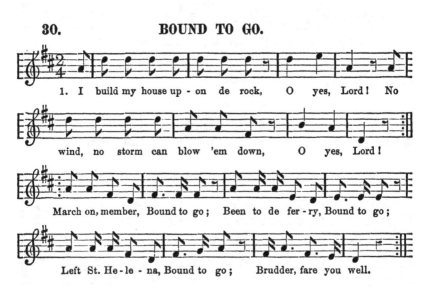

1. I build my house up - on de rock, O yes, Lord! No
wind, no storm can blow 'em down,   O   yes, Lord!
March on, member, Bound to go;   Been to de fer - ry, Bound to go;
Left St. He - le - na, Bound to go ;   Brudder, fare you well.

2 I build my house on shiftin' sand,
  De first wind come he blow him down.

3 I am not like de foolish man,
  He build his house upon de sand.

4 One mornin' as I was a walkin' along,
  I saw de berries a-hanging down.

5 I pick de berries and I suck de juice,
  He sweeter dan de honey comb.

  I tuk dem brudder, two by two,
  I tuk dem sister, tree by tree.

Variation.

I   build my house up - on   a   rock,   O   yes, Lord! No

wind nor storm shall blow dem down, O yes, Lord!

March on, member, Bound to go; March on, member, Bound to go;

March on, mem-ber, Bound to go; Bid 'em fare you well.

31. MICHAEL ROW THE BOAT ASHORE.

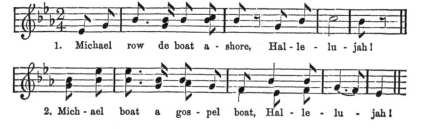

1. Michael row de boat a - shore, Hal - le - lu - jah!

2. Mich - ael boat a gos - pel boat, Hal - le - lu - jah!

3 I wonder where my mudder deh (there).

4 See my mudder on de rock gwine home.

5 On de rock gwine home in Jesus' name.

6 Michael boat a music boat.

7 Gabriel blow de trumpet horn.

8 O you mind your boastin' talk.

9 Boastin' talk will sink your soul.

10 Brudder, lend a helpin' hand.

11 Sister, help for trim dat boat.

12 Jordan stream is wide and deep.

13 Jesus stand on t' oder side.

14 I wonder if my maussa deh.

15 My fader gone to unknown land.

16 O de Lord he plant his garden deh.

24

17 He raise de fruit for you to eat.
18 He dat eat shall neber die.
19 When de riber overflow.
20 O poor sinner, how you land?
21 Riber run and darkness comin'.
22 Sinner row to save your soul.

Words from Hilton Head.

Michael haul the boat ashore.
Then you'll hear the horn they blow.
Then you'll hear the trumpet sound.
Trumpet sound the world around.
Trumpet sound for rich and poor.
Trumpet sound the jubilee.
Trumpet sound for you and me.

32.   **SAIL, O BELIEVER.**

Sail, O be-liev-er, sail, Sail o-ver yon-der;

Sail, O my brudder, sail, Sail o-ver yon-der.

[Col. Higginson gives the following stanzas, of which the above seems to be a
part; but unfortunately he is unable to identify the music, which is well described by the terms in which he speaks of the words—" very graceful and
lyrical, and with more variety of rhythm than usual:"

"Bow low, Mary, bow low, Martha,
For Jesus come and lock de door,
And carry de keys away.

Sail, sail, over yonder,
And view de promised land,
For Jesus come, &c.

Weep, O Mary, bow low, Martha,
For Jesus come, &c.

Sail, sail, my true believer;
Sail, sail, over yonder;
Mary, bow low, Martha, bow low,
For Jesus come and lock de door,
And carry de keys away."]

33.

ROCK O' JUBILEE.

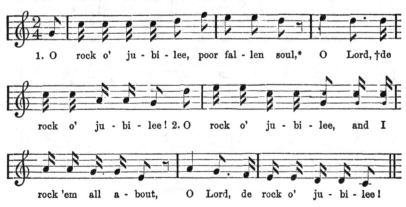

1. O rock o' ju - bi - lee, poor fal - len soul,* O Lord, †de

rock o' ju - bi - lee! 2. O rock o' ju - bi - lee, and I

rock 'em all a - bout, O Lord, de rock o' ju - bi - lee!

3 Stand back, Satan, let me come by.

4 O come, titty Katy, let me go.

5 I have no time for stay at home.

6 My Fader door wide open now.

7 Mary, girl, you know my name.

8 Look dis way an' you look dat way.

9 De wind blow East, he blow from Jesus.

* To mercy seat, To de corner o' de world. † Yes.

34. # STARS BEGIN TO FALL.

I tink I hear my brud - der *say, Call de na - tion

great and small; I look - ee on de God's right

hand, When de stars be-gin to fall. Oh what a mournin' (sis-ter),

Oh what a mourn - in' (brud - der), Oh what a

mourn - in', When de stars be - gin to fall.

* Titty Nelly, De member, &c.

35. KING EMANUEL.

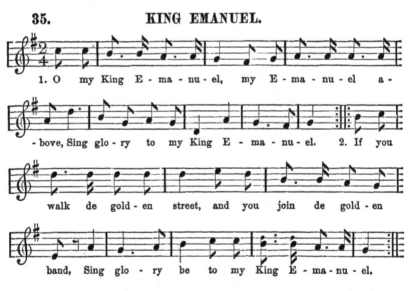

1. O my King E - ma - nu - el, my E - ma - nu - el a -

- bove, Sing glo - ry to my King E - ma - nu - el. 2. If you

walk de gold - en street, and you join de gold - en

band, Sing glo - ry be to my King E - ma - nu - el.

3 If you touch one string, den de whole heaven ring.

4 O the great cherubim, O de cherubim above.

5 O believer, ain't you glad dat your soul is converted?

[This hymn—words and melody—bears all the marks of white origin. We have not, however, been able to find it in any hymn-book, and therefore retain it, as being a favorite at Port Royal.]

36. SATAN'S CAMP A-FIRE.

Fi - er, my Sav - iour, fi - er, Sa - tan's camp a -

fire ; Fi - er, be - lie - ver, fi - er, Sa - tan's camp a - fire.

37. GIVE UP THE WORLD.

De sun give a light* in de heaven all round, De

sun give a light in de heaven all round, De

sun give a light in de heaven all round, Why

don't you give up de world? My brud-der, don't you

give up de world? My brud - der, don't you

give up de world? My brud - der, don't you

give up de world? We must leave de world be - hind.

* De moon give a light, De starry crown.

[The first movement of this air is often sung in the minor key.ɟ

38.   JESUS ON THE WATER-SIDE.

Heaven bell a - ring, I know de road, Heaven bell a-ring, I know de road ;

Heaven bell a - ring, I know de road, Je - sus sit - tin' on de

wa - ter - side. Do come a - long, do let us go,

Do come a - long, do let us go, Do come a - long, do

let us go, Je - sus sit - t.n' on de wa - ter - side.

39. I WISH I BEEN DERE.

My mud - der, you fol - low Je - sus, My

sis - ter, you fol - low Je - sus, My brudder, you fol - low Je - sus, To

fight un - til I die. I wish I been dere, To climb Ja - cob's
yonder,

lad - der, I wish I ben dere, To wear de star - ry crown.
yonder,

40. BUILD A HOUSE IN PARADISE.

My

My brud - der build a house in Pa - ra - dise,......

fader build a house | 1st | 2d |

...... O - na build a house. in Pa - ra - dise, Pa - ra - dise.

Build it wid - out a ham - mer or a nail,

Build it wid - out a ham - mer or a nail.

41. I KNOW WHEN I'M GOING HOME.

Old Satan told me to my face, O yes, Lord, De
God I seek I nev-er find, O yes, Lord. True be-
- liev - er, I know when I gwine home, True be-
- liev - er, I know when I gwine home, True be-
- liev-er, I know when I gwine home, I been a - fraid to die.

42. I'M A-TROUBLE IN DE MIND.

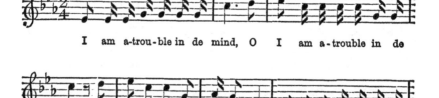

I am a-trou-ble in de mind, O I am a-trouble in de
mind; I ask my Lord what shall I do, I am a - trouble in de

mind.　　　　I'm a - trou - ble in de mind, What you

doubt for?* I'm a - trou - ble in de mind.

* Titty Rosy, Brudder Johnny, Come along dere.

43.　　　　　　**TRAVEL ON.**

Sister Ro-sy, you get to heaven be-fore I go, Sis-ter, you

look out for me, I'm on de way. Trabel on, tra-bel

on, you heaven-born soldier, Tra-bel on, tra-bel,

on, Go hear - de what my Je - sus say.

* Heaven-bound.

44. ARCHANGEL OPEN THE DOOR.

I ax all dem brud - der* roun', Brudder,* why
can't you pray for me? I ax all dem
brudder roun', Brudder, why can't you pray for me? 1. I'm
gwine to my heaven, I'm gwine home, Arch-an-gel o - pen de door; I'm
gwine to my heaven, I'm gwine home; Arch-an - gel o pen de door.

2 Brudder, tuk off your knapsack, I'm gwine home;
Archangel open de door.

* Sister.

45. MY BODY ROCK 'LONG FEVER.

1. Wai', my brudder, * bet-ter true believe, † Better true be long time
get o - ver cros-ses; Wai', my sis - ter, bet-ter true be-lievc, An' 'e

get up to heaven at last. O my bo-dy rock 'long fev-er, O!

wid a pain in 'e head! I wish I been to de

king-dom, to sit a - long side o' my Lord!

2 By de help ob de Lord we rise up again,
O de Lord he comfort de sinner :
By de help ob de Lord we rise up again,
An' we'll get to heaven at last.

* All de member.　　　　　† Long time seeker 'gin to believe.

Variation.

O my body's racked wid de fe-ve-er, My head rack'd wid de

pain I hab, I wish I was in de king-do-om, A-

- set - tin' on de side ob de Lord.

[This is one of the most striking of the Port Royal spirituals, and is shown by a comparison with No. 93 to be one of the most widely spread of all the African hymns. It is hard to explain every word of the introduction, but "long time get over crosses" is of course the "long time waggin' o' er de crossin'" of the Virginia hymn.]

46. BELL DA RING.

I know member, know Lord, I know I yed - de de
bell da ring. 1. Want to go to meet - ing, Bell da ring,
Want to go to meet-ing, Bell da ring. 2. (Say) Road so storm - y,*
Bell da ring, (Say) Road so storm - y, Bell da ring.

3 I can't get to meetin'. †
4 De church mos' ober.
5 De heaven-bell a heaven-bell.
6 De heaven-bell I gwine home.
7 I shout for de heaven-bell.
8 Heaven 'nough for me one.
9 (Brudder) hain't you a member?

* Boggy, Tedious.   † 'ciety, Lecter, Praise-house.

[The following words were sung in Col. Higginson's regiment:

Do my brudder, O yes, yes, member,
    De bell done ring.
You can't get to heaben
    When de bell done ring.
If you want to get to heaven,
    Fo' de bell, etc
You had better follow Jesus,
    Fo' de bell, etc.
O yes, my Jesus, yes, I member,
    De bell etc.
O come in, Christians,
    Fo' de bell, etc.
For the gates are all shut,
    When de bell, etc.
And you can't get to heaben
    When de bell, etc.

Col. Higginson suggests that this refrain may have originated in Virginia, and gone South with our army, because "'done' is a Virginia shibboleth, quite distinct from the 'been' which replaces it in South Carolina. In the proper South Carolina dialect, would have been substituted 'De bell been-a-ring.'" We have, however, shown in the preface, that "done" is used on St. Helena; and at any rate the very general use of this refrain there in the present tense, "Bell da ring," would indicate that it was of local origin, while we have never met with anything at all like it in any other part of the country. As given above, it is one of the most characteristic "shouting" tunes.

In singing "Heaven-bell a heaven-bell," the *v* and *n* were so run together that the words sounded like "hum-bell a hum-bell," with a strong emphasis and dwelling upon the *m*.]

47.   PRAY ALL DE MEMBER.

1. Pray all de mem-ber,* O Lord! Pray all de mem-ber,
Yes, my Lord! 2. Pray a lit-tle lon-ger, O Lord!
Pray a lit-tle lon-ger, Yes, my Lord! 3. Je-ri-cho da wor-ry me,
O Lord! Je-ri-cho da wor-ry me, Yes, my Lord!

4   Jericho, Jericho.
5   I been to Jerusalem.
6   Patrol aroun' me.
7   Tank God he no ketch me.
8   Went to de meetin'.
9   Met brudder Hacless [Hercules].
10   Wha' d'ye tink he tell me?
11   Tell me for to turn back.
12   Jump along Jericho.

* True believer.

[This also is a very characteristic shouting tune.]

48.   TURN, SINNER, TURN O!

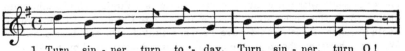

1. Turn, sin - ner, turn to - day, Turn, sin - ner, turn O!
2. Turn, O sin - ner, de worl' da gwine, Turn, sin - ner, turn O!

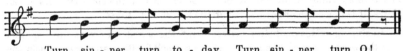

Turn, sin - ner, turn to - day, Turn, sin - ner, turn O!
Turn, O sin - ner, de worl' da gwine, Turn, sin - ner, turn O!

1st var.

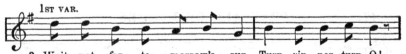

3. Wait not for to - morrow's sun, Turn, sin - ner, turn O!
4. To-morrow's sun will sure to shine, Turn, sin - ner, turn O!

Wait not for to - morrow's sun, Turn, sin - ner, turn O!
To-morrow's sun will sure to shine, Turn, sin - ner, turn O!

2d var.

5. The sun may shine, but on your grave, Turn, sinner, turn O!   The

sun may shine, but on your grave, Turn, sin - ner, turn O!

3d var.

6. Hark! I hear dem sin - ner say, Turn, sin - ner, turn O!
7. If you get to heaven I'll get there too, Turn, sin - ner, turn O!

Hark! I hear dem sin - ner say, Turn, sin - ner, turn O!
If you get to heaven I'll get there too, Turn, sin - ner, turn O!

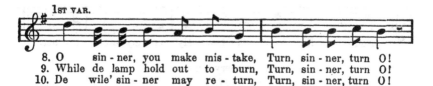

8. O sin - ner, you make mis - take, Turn, sin - ner, turn O!
9. While de lamp hold out to burn, Turn, sin - ner, turn O!
10. De wile' sin - ner may re - turn, Turn, sin - ner, turn O!

O sin - ner, you make mis - take, Turn, sin - ner, turn O!
While de lamp hold out to burn, Turn, sin - ner, turn O!
De wile' sin - ner may re - turn, Turn, sin - ner, turn O!

The following words are sung to the same tune :

1 Bro' Joe, you ought to know my name--Hallelujah.

2 My name is written in de book ob life.

3 If you look in de book you'll fin' 'em dar.

4 One mornin' I was a walkin' down.

5 I saw de berry a-hinging down.

6 (Lord) I pick de berry, an' I suck de juice.

7 Jes' as sweet as de honey in de comb.

8 I wonder where fader Jimmy gone.

9 My fader gone to de yonder worl'.

10 You dig de spring dat nebber dry.

11 De more I dig 'em, de water spring.

12 De water spring dat nebber dry.

[This is the most dramatic of all the shouts ; the tune varies with the words, commonly about as given above, and the general effect is very pathetic. The words and tunes are constantly interchanged : thus, for instance, the 6th verse might be sung to the second variation, and the 8th, 9th and 10th, to the third.]

49. **MY ARMY CROSS OVER.**

1. My brudder, tik keer Sa-tan, My ar-my cross o-ber, My

brud-der, tik keer Sa-tan, My ar-my cross o-ber.

2 Satan bery busy.

3 Wash 'e face in ashes.

4 Put on de leder apron.

5 Jordan riber rollin'.

6 Cross 'em, I tell ye, cross 'em.

7 Cross Jordan (danger) riber.

[The following version, probably from Sapelo Id., Georgia, was sung in Col. Higginson's regiment:

1. My ar-my cross o-ber, My ar-my cross o-ber, O

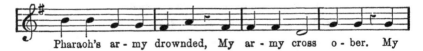

Pharaoh's ar-my drownded, My ar-my cross o-ber. My

ar-my, my ar-my, my ar-my cross o-ber.

2 We'll cross de riber Jordan.

3 We'll cross de danger water.

4 We'll cross de mighty Myo.

[On the word "Myo," Col. Higginson makes the following note: "I could get no explanation of the 'mighty Myo,' except that one of the old men thought it meant the river of death. Perhaps it is an African word. In the Cameroon dialect, 'Mawa' signifies 'to die.'" Lt. Col. Trowbridge feels very confident that it is merely a corruption of "bayou."]

50. **JOIN THE ANGEL BAND.**

1. If you look up de road you see fa- der Mose-y,
Join de an-gel band, If you look up de road you
see fa - der Mose-y, Join de an - gel band.

2 Do, fader Mosey, gader your army.

3 O do mo' soul gader togeder.

4 O do join 'em, join 'em for Jesus.

5 O do join 'em, join 'em archangel.

The following variation of the first line, with the words that follow, was sung in Charleston :

O join 'em all, join for Je - sus.

O join 'em all, join for Jesus, Join Jerusalem Band.

Sister Mary, stan' up for Jesus.

Sixteen souls set out for Heaven.

O brudder an' sister, come up for Heaven.

Daddy Peter set out for Jesus.

Ole Maum Nancy set out for Heaven.

[" The South Carolina negroes never say Aunty and Uncle to old persons, but Daddy and Maumer, and all the white people say Daddy and Maumer to old black men and women "—A. M. B.

This is no doubt correct as regards South Carolina in general. I am sure that I heard "Uncle" and "Aunty" at Port Royal, and I do not remember hearing " Daddy " and " Maumer."—W. F. A.]

51.　　　I AN' SATAN HAD A RACE.

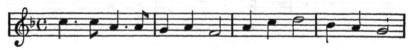

1. I　an' Sa - tan　had a　race, Hal - le - lu,　hal - le - lu,

I　an' Sa - tan had a　race, Hal - le - lu,　hal - le - lu

2 Win de race agin de course.

3 Satan tell me to my face

4 He will break my kingdom down.

5 Jesus whisper in my heart

6 He will build 'em up again.

7 Satan mount de iron grey ;

8 Ride half way to Pilot-Bar.

9 Jesus mount de milk-white horse.

10 Say you cheat my fader children.

11 Say you cheat 'em out of glory.

12 Trouble like a gloomy cloud

13 Gader dick an' tundor loud.

52. SHALL I DIE?

1. Be - liev - er, O shall I die? O my ar - my, shall I die?

2. Je - sus die, shall I die? Die on the cross, shall I die?

3 Die, die, die, shall I die?
Jesus da coming, shall I die?

4 Run for to meet him, shall I die?
Weep like a weeper, shall I die?

5 Mourn like a mourner, shall I die?
Cry like a crier, shall I die?

[This shout was a great favorite on the Capt. John Fripp plantation; its simplicity, wildness and minor character suggest a native African origin. Sometimes the leading singer would simply repeat the words, mournfully: "Die, die, die,"—sometimes he would interpolate such an inappropriate line as "Jump along, jump along dere."]

53. WHEN WE DO MEET AGAIN.

When we do meet a - gain, When we do meet a - gain, When we

do meet a - gain, 'Twill be no more to part.

Broth - er Bil - ly, fare you well, Broth - er Bil - ly,

fare you well, We'll sing hal - le - lu - jah, when we do meet a - gain.

54. THE WHITE MARBLE STONE.

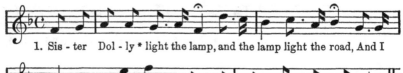

1. Sis - ter Dol - ly * light the lamp, and the lamp light the road, And I

wish I been there for to yed - de Jor - dan roll.

2 O the city light the lamp, the white man he will sold,
And I wish I been there, etc.

3 O the white marble stone, and the white marble stone.

* Believer, Patty, etc.

[This song was described to us as "*too* pretty." The following minor variation might be called "too *much* prettier."

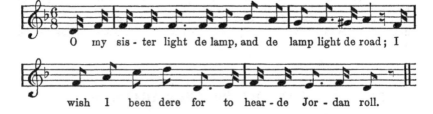

O my sis - ter light de lamp, and de lamp light de road; I

wish I been dere for to hear - de Jor - dan roll.

55. I CAN'T STAND THE FIRE.

I can't stan' de fire, (dear sister) I can't stan' de fire, (O Lord) I

can't stan' de fire, While Jordan da roll so swif'. (Tiddy 'Rinah.)

[Probably only a fragment of a longer piece. The following variation was sung at Coffin's Point:

Can't stand the fire, Can't stand the fire, Can't, etc. (O Lord, I) Can't stand the fire.

56. **MEET, O LORD!**

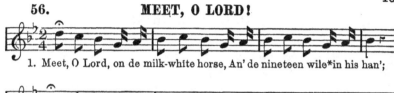

1. Meet, O Lord, on de milk-white horse, An' de nineteen wile*in his han';

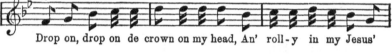

Drop on, drop on de crown on my head, An' roll-y in my Jesus'

arm. In dat mornin' all day, In dat mornin' all day,

In dat mornin' all day, When Je-sus de Chris' been born.

2 Moon went into de poplar tree,
  An' star went into blood ;
  In dat mornin', etc.

* *i. e.* the anointing vial.

[This was taught me by a boy from Hilton Head Island, whom the rebel Gen. Drayton left holding his horse "when gun shoot at Bay Pint." The General never returned to reclaim his horse, which afterwards came into the possession of a friend of mine, and was famed for swiftness. I had several fine rides upon "milk-white" *Drayton.—*W. F. A.]

57. **WAIT, MR. MACKRIGHT.**

Wai', Mister Mackright, an' 'e yed-de what Sa-tan

say: Satan full me full of music, an' tell me not to pray.

Mister Mackright cry ho-ly; O Lord, cry ho-ly.

58.   **EARLY IN THE MORNING.**

Variation.

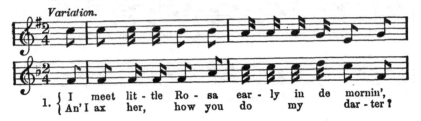

1. { I meet lit-tle Ro-sa ear-ly in de mornin',
An' I ax her, how you do my dar-ter?

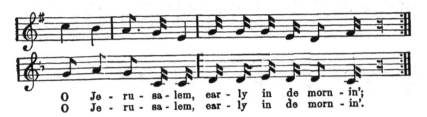

O Je-ru-sa-lem, ear-ly in de morn-in';
O Je-ru-sa-lem, ear-ly in de morn-in'.

Walk 'em eas-y round de heaben, Walk 'em easy round de heaben,

Walk 'em easy round de heaben, Till all living may join dat band.*

2 I meet my mudder early in de mornin',
  An' I ax her, how you do my mudder?
    Walk 'em easy, etc.

3 I meet brudder Robert early in de mornin';
  I ax brudder Robert, how you do, my sonny?

4 I meet titta-Wisa † early in de mornin';
  I ax titta-Wisa, how you do, my darter?

* O shout glory till 'em join dat ban'.   † *i. e.* sister Louisa.

["This shout is accompanied by the peculiar shuffling dance, except in the chorus, where they walk around in slow time, keeping step to their song."— J. S. R.]

59. **HAIL, MARY.**

I want some valiant soldier here, I want some valiant

soldier here, I want some valiant sol - dier here, To

help me bear de cross. O hail, Mary, hail! O hail, Mary,

hail! O hail, Ma - ry, hail! To help me bear de cross.

["I fancied," says Col. Higginson, "that the original reading might have been 'soul,' instead of 'soldier,'—with some other syllable inserted, to fill out the metre,—and that the 'Hail, Mary,' might denote a Roman Catholic origin, as I had several men from St. Augustine who held in a dim way to that faith."

In Mr. Spaulding's article in the *Continental Monthly*, a tune nearly identical with this is given with words almost the same as those of "No more peck of corn," No. 64, the whole as an introduction to the second part of "Trouble of the World," No. 10—a curious illustration of the way in which the colored people make different combinations of their own tunes at different times :]

1. Done wid dri - ber's dri - bin', Done wid dri - ber's

dri - bin', Done wid driber's dri - bin', Roll, Jordan, roll.

2 Done wid massa's hollerin',

3 Done wid missus' scoldin'.

60. **NO MORE RAIN FALL FOR WET YOU.**

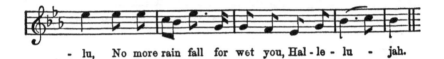

1. No more rain fall for wet you, Hal - le - lu, hal - le -

- lu, No more rain fall for wet you, Hal - le - lu - jah.

2 No more sun shine for burn you.

3 No more parting in de kingdom.

4 No more backbiting in de kingdom.

5 Every day shall be Sunday.

61. **I WANT TO GO HOME.**

In chanting style.

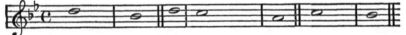

1. Dere's no rain to | wet you. ‖ O | yes, I want to go | home, ‖ Want to go | home. ‖

2 Dere's no sun to burn you,—O yes, etc.

3 Dere's no hard trials.

4 Dere's no whips a-crackin'.

5 Dere's no stormy weather.

6 Dere's no tribulation.

7 No more slavery in de kingdom.

8 No evil-doers in de kingdom.

9 All is gladness in de kingdom.

[Verse 7 was added after the Emancipation Proclamation.—J. S. R.]

62.   **GOOD-BYE, BROTHER.**

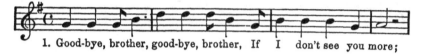

1. Good-bye, brother, good-bye, brother, If I don't see you more;

Now God bless you, now God bless you, If I don't see you more.

2 We part in de body but we meet in de spirit,
We'll meet in de heaben in de blessed * kingdom.

3 So good-bye, brother, good-bye, sister ;
Now God bless you, now God bless you.

* Glorious.

["Sung at the breaking up of a midnight meeting after the death of a soldier. These midnight *wails* are very solemn to me, and exhibit the sadness of the present mingled with the joyful hope of the future. I have known the negroes to get together in groups of six or eight around a small fire, and sing and pray alternately from nine o'clock till three the next morning, after the death of one of their number."—J. S. R.]

63.   **FARE YE WELL.**

O fare you well, my brudder, fare you well by de

grace of God, For I'se gwin-en home; I'se gwin-en

home, my Lord, I'se gwinen home. Mas-sa Je-sus gib me a

48

lit - tle   broom, For to sweep my heart clean;

Sweep 'em clean by de grace of God, An' glo - ry in my soul.

64.   **MANY THOUSAND GO.**

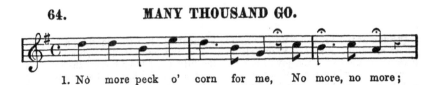

1. No more peck o' corn for me, No more, no more;

No more peck o' corn for me, Man - y tousand go.

2 No more driver's lash for me.

3 No more pint o' salt for me.

4 No more hundred lash for me.

5 No more mistress' call for me.

[A song " to which the Rebellion had actually given rise. This was composed by nobody knows whom—though it was the most recent doubtless of all these 'spirituals.'—and had been sung in secret to avoid detection. It is certainly plaintive enough. The peck of corn and pint of salt were slavery's rations."— T. W. H. Lt. Col. Trowbridge learned that it was first sung when Beauregard took the slaves of the islands to build the fortifications at Hilton Head and Bay Point.]

65. BROTHER MOSES GONE.

Brud - der Mo - ses gone to de promised. land,

Hal - le - lu, hal - le - lu - jah.

66. THE SIN-SICK SOUL.

Brudder George is a - gwine to glo - ry, Take

car' de sin - sick soul, Brudder George is a - gwine to

glo - ry, Take car' de sin - sick soul. Brudder

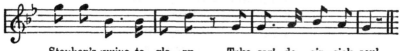

Stephen's gwine to glo - ry, Take car' de sin - sick soul.

50

67.　　　　**SOME VALIANT SOLDIER.**

Oh Lord, I want some va - li - ant sol - dier, I

want some va - li - ant sol - dier, I want some valiant

soldier, To help me bear de cross. For I weep, I weep, I

can't hold out; If a - ny mer - cy, Lord, O pit - y poor me.

[The words are in part the same as those of " Hail Mary," No. 59.]

68.　　　　**HALLELU, HALLELU.**

1. Oh one day as an - od - er, Hal - le - lu, hal - le -

- lu! 2. When de ship is out a - sail - in', Hal - le - lu - jah!

3 Member walk and never tire.

4 Member walk Jordan long road.

5 Member walk tribulation.

6 You go home to Wappoo.

7 Member seek new repentance.

8 I go to seek my fortune.

9 I go to seek my dying Saviour.

10 You want to die like Jesus.

[For other words, see " Children do linger," No. 69.]

69. CHILDREN DO LINGER.

1. O member, will you lin - ger? See de chil - 'en do

lin - ger here. 2. I go to glo - ry wid you, Member, join.

3 O Jesus is our Captain.

4 He lead us on to glory.

5 We'll meet at Zion gateway.*

6 We'll talk dis story over.

7 We'll enter into glory.

8 When we done wid dis world trials.

9 We done wid all our crosses.

10 O brudder, will you meet us?

11 When de ship is out a-sailin'.

12 O Jesus got de hellum.

13 Fader, gader in your chil'en.

14 O gader dem for Zion.

15 'Twas a beauteous Sunday mornin'.

16 When he rose from de dead.

17 He will bring you milk and honey.

* Heaven portal.

70. **GOOD-BYE.**

Good-bye, my brudder, good-bye, Hal - le - lu - jah! Good-bye, sister Sal - ly, good-bye, Hal - le - lu - jah! Go - ing home, Hal - le - lu - jah! Je - sus call me, Hal - le - lu - jah! Lin - ger no longer, Hal - le - lu - jah! Tar - ry no' longer, Hal - le - lu - jah!

[" This is sung at the breaking up of a meeting, with a general shaking of hands, and the name of him or her pronounced, whose hand is shaken ; of course there is seeming confusion."—Mrs. C. J. B.]

71. **LORD, MAKE ME MORE PATIENT.**

Lord, make me more patient,* Lord, make me more pa - tient, Lord, make me more pa - tient, Un - til we meet a - gain; Pa - tient, pa - tient, pa - tient, Un - til we meet a - gain.

* " Any adjective expressive of the virtues is inserted here: holy, loving, peaceful, etc."—Mrs. C. J. B.

72. ## THE DAY OF JUDGMENT.

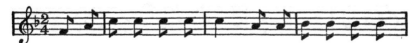

1. And de moon will turn to   blood, And de moon will turn to

blood, And de moon will turn to blood In dat day—O-yoy,* my

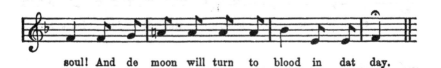

soul! And de moon will turn to blood in dat day.

2 And you'll see de stars a-fallin'.

3 And de world will be on fire.

4 And you'll hear de saints a-singin :

5 And de Lord will say to de sheep.

6 For to go to Him right hand ;

7 But de goats must go to de left.

* "A sort of prolonged wail."—Mrs. C. J. B.

73. THE RESURRECTION MORN.

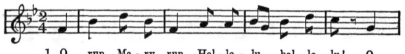

1. O run, Ma - ry, run, Hal - le - lu, hal - le - lu! O

run, Ma - ry, run, Hal - le - lu - jah! 2. It was

ear - ly in de morn - in', Hal - le - lu, hal - le -

- lu! It was ear - ly in de mornin', Hal - le - lu - jah!

3 That she went to de sepulchre,

4 And de Lord he wasn't da.

5 But she see a man a-comin',

6 And she thought it was de gardener.

7 But he say, " O touch me not,

8 " For I am not yet ascended.

9 " But tell to my disciples

10 " Dat de Lord he is arisen."

11 So run, Mary, run, etc.

74. NOBODY KNOWS THE TROUBLE I'VE HAD.

No - bod - y knows de trouble I've had,* No - bod - y knows but Je - sus, No - bod - y knows de trouble I've had, (Sing) Glo - ry hal - le - lu! 1. One morning I was a - walking down, O yes, Lord! I saw some ber - ries a - hanging down,

Variation on St. Helena Id.

O yes, Lord! O yes, Lord! I saw some berries hanging down.

2 I pick de berry and I suck de juice, O yes, Lord!
  Just as sweet as the honey in de comb, O yes, Lord!

3 Sometimes I'm up, sometimes I'm down,
  Sometimes I'm almost on de groun'.

4 What make ole Satan hate me so?
  Because he got me once and he let me go.

* I see.

[This song was a favorite in the colored schools of Charleston in 1865; it has since that time spread to the Sea Islands, where it is now sung with the variation noted above. An independent transcription of this melody, sent from Florida by Lt. Col. Apthorp, differed only in the ictus of certain measures, as has also been noted above. The third verse was furnished by Lt. Col. Apthorp. Once when there had been a good deal of ill feeling excited, and trouble was apprehended, owing to the uncertain action of Government in regard to the confiscated lands on the Sea Islands, Gen. Howard was called upon to address the colored people earnestly and even severely. Sympathizing with them, however, he could not speak to his own satisfaction; and to relieve their minds of the ever-present sense of injustice, and prepare them to listen, he asked them to sing. Immediately an old woman on the outskirts of the meeting began "Nobody knows the trouble I've had," and the whole audience joined in. The General was so affected by the plaintive words and melody, that he found himself melting into tears and quite unable to maintain his official sternness.]

75.   WHO IS ON THE LORD'S SIDE.

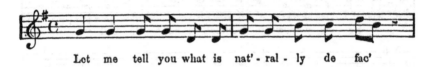

Let me tell you what is nat'-ral-ly de fac'

Who is on de Lord's side, None o' God's chil-'n

neb-ber look back, Who is on de Lord's side.

1. Way in de wal-ley, Who is on de Lord's side,

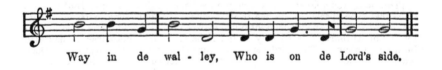

Way in de wal-ley, Who is on de Lord's side.

2 Weepin' Mary.

3 Mournin' Marta.

4 Risen Jesus.

76. **HOLD OUT TO THE END.**

All dem Mount Zion member, dey have many ups and downs; But

cross come or no come, for to hold out to the end.

Hold out to the end, hold out to the end, It

is my 'ter - mi - na - tion for to hold out to the end.

77. **COME GO WITH ME.**

1. Ole Satan is a bus- y ole man, He roll stones in my

way; Mass' Jesus is my bo - som friend, He roll 'em out o' my

58

way. O come-e go wid me, O come-e go wid me,

O come-e go wid me, A - walkin' in de heaven I roam.

2 I did not come here myself, my Lord,
It was my Lord who brought me here;
And I really do believe I'm a child of God,
A-walkin' in de heaven I roam.
O come-e go wid me, etc.

78.   **EVERY HOUR IN THE DAY.**

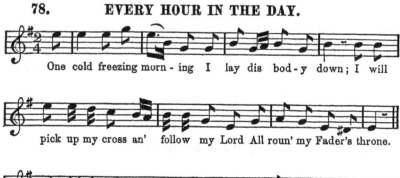

One cold freezing morn - ing I lay dis bod-y down; I will

pick up my cross an' follow my Lord All roun' my Fader's throne.

1. Every hour in de day cry ho - ly, Cry ho-ly, my Lord! Every

hour in de day cry ho - ly, Oh show me de crime I've done.

2 Every hour in de night cry Jesus, etc.

79. **IN THE MANSIONS ABOVE.**

Good Lord, in de manshans a - bove, Good Lord, in de

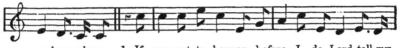

manshans above, My Lord, I hope to meet my Je - sus In de

manshans above. 1. If you get to heaven before I do, Lord, tell my

Je - sus I'm a - comin' too, To de man - shans a - bove.

2 My Lord, I've had many crosses an' trials here below;
    My Lord, I hope to meet you
        In de manshans above.

3 Fight on, my brudder, for de manshans above,
    For I hope to meet my Jesus dere
        In de manshans above.

80.   ### SHOUT ON, CHILDREN.

1. Shout on, chil'en, you nev - er die; Glo - ry hal - le - lu!

You in de Lord, an' de Lord in you; Glo - ry hal - le - lu!

2 Shout an' pray both night an' day;
   How can you die, you in de Lord?

3 Come on, chil'en, let's go home;
   O I'm so glad you're in de Lord.

81.   ### JESUS, WON'T YOU COME BY-AND-BYE?

You ride dat horse, you call him Mac - a - do - ni,

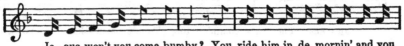

Je - sus, won't you come bumby? You ride him in de mornin' and you

ride him in de evenin', Je - sus, won't you come bumby?   De

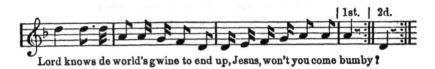

Lord knows de world's gwine to end up, Jesus, won't you come bumby?

82.   **HEAVE AWAY.**

Heave a - way, heave a - way! I'd rather court a yellow gal than

work for Hen - ry Clay. Heave a - way,   heave a -

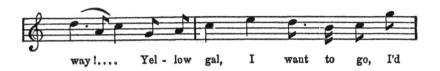

way!.... Yel - low gal,   I   want   to   go,   I'd

rath - er court a yel - low gal than work for Hen - ry Clay.

Heave a - way!   Yel - low gal,   I   want   to   go!

[This is one of the Savannah firemen's songs of which Mr. Kane O'Donnel
gave a graphic account in a letter to the Philadelphia *Press.* "Each company,"
he says, "has its own set of tunes, its own leader, and doubtless in the growth
of time, necessity and invention, its own composer."]

II.

NORTHERN SEABOARD SLAVE STATES:

Including Delaware, Maryland, Virginia, and North Carolina.

SLAVE SONGS OF THE UNITED STATES.

II.

83. **WAKE UP, JACOB.**

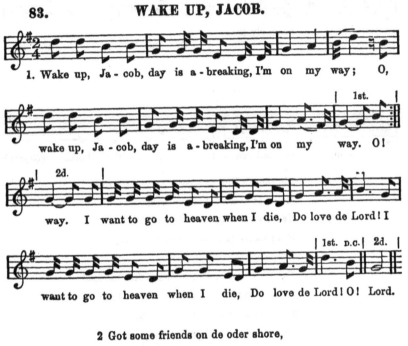

1. Wake up, Ja - cob, day is a - breaking, I'm on my way; O,
wake up, Ja - cob, day is a - breaking, I'm on my way. O!
way. I want to go to heaven when I die, Do love de Lord! I
want to go to heaven when I die, Do love de Lord! O! Lord.

2 Got some friends on de oder shore,
    Do love de Lord!
  I want to see 'em more an' more,
    Do love de Lord!
      Wake up, Jacob, &c.

84.   **ON TO GLORY.**

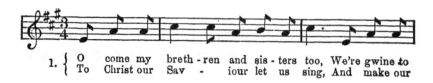

1. { O come my breth-ren and sis-ters too, We're gwine to
To Christ our Sav - iour let us sing, And make our

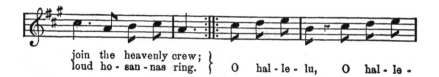

join the heavenly crew; }
loud ho-san-nas ring. } O hal-le-lu, O hal-le-

- lu, O hal-le-lu-jah to the Lord. (*Repeat.*)

2 Oh, there's Bill Thomas, I know him well,
  He's got to work to keep from hell;
  He's got to pray by night and day,
  If he wants to go by the narrow way.

3 There's Chloe Williams, she makes me mad,
  For you see I know she's going on bad;
  She told me a lie this arternoon,
  And the devil will get her very soon.

[We should be tempted, from the character of this tune, to doubt its genuineness as a pure negro song. We are informed, however, that it was sung
twenty-five years ago in negro camp-meetings, and not in those of the whites.
The words, at any rate, are worth preserving, as illustrating the kind of influence brought to bear upon the wavering.]

85.   **JUST NOW.**

1. Sanc - to - fy   me,   sanc - to - fy   me,   Sanc - to -

- fy   me,   sanc - to - fy   me,   Sanc - to - fy   me,   just

now;   Just now ;   just now ;   Sancto - fy   me   just now.

2 Good religion, good religion, etc.

3 Come to Jesus, come to Jesus, etc.

[This, which is now, in a somewhat different form, a Methodist hymn, was sung as given above, by the colored people of Ann Arundel Co., Md., twenty-five years ago.—W. A. H.]

86.   **SHOCK ALONG, JOHN.**

Shock along, John, shock along.

Shock along, John, shock along.

[A corn-song, of which only the burden is remembered.]

87.   **ROUND THE CORN, SALLY.**

1. Five can't ketch me and ten can't hold me,   Ho,......

round the corn,   Sal - ly !   Round the corn,   round the corn,

round the corn, Sal - ly !   Ho, ho, ho, round the corn, Sal - ly !

2 Here's your iggle-quarter and here's your count-aquils.

3 I can bank, 'ginny bank, 'ginny bank the weaver.

["Iggle" is of course "eagle;" for the rest of the enigmatical words and expressions in this coru-song, we must leave readers to guess at the interpretation.]

88.   **JORDAN'S MILLS.**

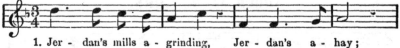

1. Jer - dan's mills a - grinding,   Jer - dan's   a - hay ;

Jer - dan's mills a - grinding,   Jer - dan's   a - hay.

2 Built without nail or hammer.

3 Runs without wind or water.

89. SABBATH HAS NO END.

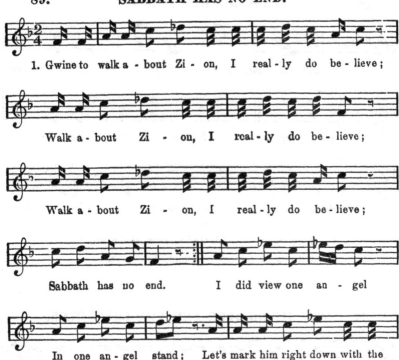

1. Gwine to walk a - bout Zi - on, I real-ly do be - lieve;

Walk a - bout Zi - on, I real-ly do be - lieve;

Walk a - bout Zi - on, I real - ly do be - lieve;

Sabbath has no end. I did view one an - gel

In one an - gel stand; Let's mark him right down with the

fore - half, With the har - pess in his hand.

2 Gwine to follow King Jesus, I really do believe.

3 I love God certain.

4 My sister's got religion.

5 Set down in the kingdom.

6 Religion is a fortune.

[This chorus was written down as exactly as possible from the lips of the singer, and illustrates the odd transformations which words undergo in their mouths. It is a verse of a familiar hymn : "fore-half" is "forehead ;" "harpess" is " harp."]

90. ## I DON'T FEEL WEARY.

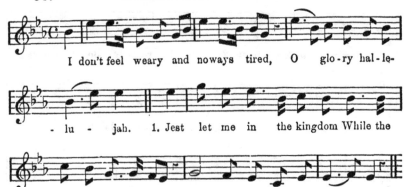

I don't feel weary and noways tired, O glo-ry hal-le-lu - jah. 1. Jest let me in the kingdom While the world is all on fire. O glo-ry hal-le-lu - jah.

2 Gwine to live with God forever, While, etc.

3 And keep the ark a-moving, While, etc.

91. ## THE HYPOCRITE AND THE CONCUBINE.

1. Hypo-crite and the concu-bine, Liv-in' among the swine, They

run to God with the lips and tongue, And leave all the heart behind.

Aunty, did you hear when Jesus rose? Did you hear when Jesus rose?

Aunty, did you hear when Jesus rose? He rose and he 'scend on high.

92. O SHOUT AWAY.

O shout, O shout, O shout a - way, And don't you mind, And

glo ry, glo - ry, glo - ry in my soul! 1. And

when 'twas night I thought 'twas day, I thought I'd pray my

soul a - way, And glo - ry, glo - ry, glo - ry in my soul!

2 O Satan told me not to pray,
He want my soul at judgment day.

3 And every where I went to pray,
There some thing was in my way.

93.   O'ER THE CROSSING.

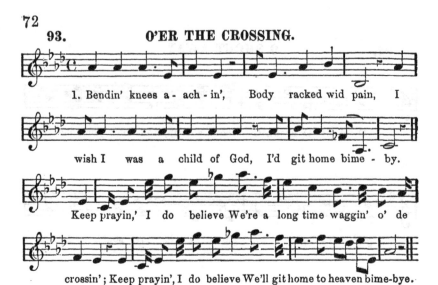

1. Bendin' knees a-ach-in', Body racked wid pain, I
wish I was a child of God, I'd git home bime-by.
Keep prayin,' I do believe We're a long time waggin' o' de
crossin'; Keep prayin', I do believe We'll git home to heaven bime-bye.

2 O yonder's my ole mudder, Been a waggin' at de hill so long;
It's about time she cross over, Git home bime-by.
    Keep prayin', I do believe, etc.

3 O hear dat lumberin' thunder A-roll from do' to do',
A-callin' de people home to God; Dey'll git home bime-by.
    Little chil'n, I do believe, etc.

4 O see dat forked lightnin' A-jump from cloud to cloud,
A-pickin' up God's chil'n; Dey'll git home bime-by.
    Pray mourner, I do believe, etc.

[This "infinitely quaint description of the length of the heavenly road," as
Col. Higginson styles it, is one of the most peculiar and wide-spread of the
spirituals. It was sung as given above in Caroline Co., Virginia, and probably
spread southward from this State. variously modified in different localities.
"My body rock 'long fever," (No. 45.) would hardly be recognised as the same,
either by words or tune, and yet it is almost certainly the same, as is shown by
the following, sung in Augusta, Georgia, which has some of the words of the
present song, adapted to a tune which is unmistakably identical with No. 45.]

O yonder's my ole mother, Been a-waggin' at de hill so long; I
really do believe she's a child of God, She'll git home to heav'n bime-bye.

[We regret we have not the air of the Nashville variation, "My Lord called
Daniel."]

94. ROCK O' MY SOUL.

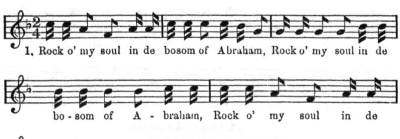

1. Rock o' my soul in de bosom of Abraham, Rock o' my soul in de bo-som of A - braham, Rock o' my soul in de bosom of A - braham, Lord, Rock o' my soul. (King Jesus.)

2 He toted the young lambs in his bosom, (ter)
And leave the old sheep alone.

95. WE WILL MARCH THROUGH THE VALLEY.

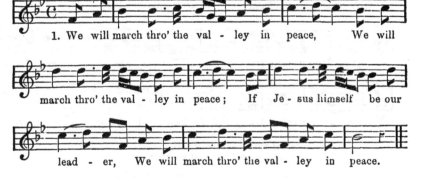

1. We will march thro' the val - ley in peace, We will march thro' the val - ley in peace; If Je - sus himself be our lead - er, We will march thro' the val - ley in peace.

2 We will march, etc.
Behold I give myself away, and
We will march, etc.

3 We will march, etc.
This track I'll see and I'll pursue;
We will march, etc.

4 We will march, etc.
When I'm dead and buried in the cold silent tomb,
I don't want you to grieve for me.

74

96.   ## WHAT A TRYING TIME.

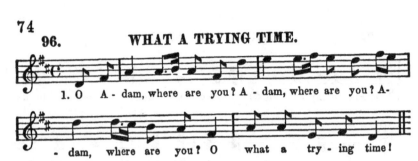

1. O A-dam, where are you? A-dam, where are you? A-dam, where are you? O what a try-ing time!

2 Lord, I am in the garden.
8 Adam, you ate that apple.
4 Lord, Eve she gave it to me.
5 Adam, it was forbidden.
6 Lord said, walk out de garden.

[A most compendious account of the fall.]

97.   ## ALMOST OVER.

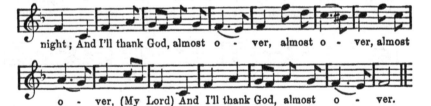

1. Some seek de Lord and they don't seek him right, Pray all day and sleep all night; And I'll thank God, almost o-ver, almost o-ver, almost o-ver, (My Lord) And I'll thank God, almost o-ver.

2 Sister, if your heart is warm,
Snow and ice will do you no harm.

8 I done been down, and I done been tried,
I been through the water, and I been baptized.

4 O sister, you must mind how you step on the cross,
Your foot might slip, and your soul get lost.

5 And when you get to heaven, you'll be able for to tell
How you shunned the gates of hell.

6 Wrestle with Satan and wrestle with sin,
Stepped over hell and come back agin.

[A baptismal song, as the chattering "almost o-ver" so forcibly suggests.]

98. **DON'T BE WEARY, TRAVELLER.**

Don't be wear - y, trav - el - ler, Come a - long home to

Je - sus; Don't be wear - y, trav - el - ler,

Come a - long home to Je - sus. 1 My head got wet with the

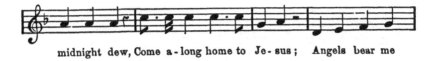

midnight dew, Come a - long home to Je - sus; Angels bear me

wit - ness too, Come a - long home to Je - sus.

2 Where to go I did not know
Ever since he freed my soul,

3 I look at de worl' and de worl' look new,
I look at de worl' and de worl' look new.

76

99.   **LET GOD'S SAINTS COME IN.**

Come down, angel, and trouble the wa-ter, Come down, angel, and

trouble the water, Come down, angel, and trouble the water, And

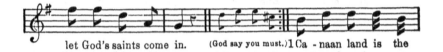

let God's saints come in.   (God say you must.) 1 Ca - naan land is the

land for me, And let God's saints come in.   Canaan land is the

land   for   me,   And   let God's saints come in.

2 There was a wicked man,
   He kept them children in Egypt land.

3 God did say to Moses one day,
   Say, Moses go to Egypt land,

4 And tell him to let my people go.
   And Pharaoh would not let 'em go.

5 God did go to Moses' house,
   And God did tell him who he was,

6 God and Moses walked and talked,
   And God did show him who he was.

100. THE GOLDEN ALTAR.

John saw-r-O, John saw-r-O... John saw de ho-ly number

set - tin' on de gold - en al - tar! 1. It's a

lit-tle while longer yere below, yere below, yere be-low, It's a

lit-tle while longer yere be-low, Be-fore de Lamb of God!

2 And home to Jesus we will go, we will go, etc.;
   We are de people of de Lord.
      John sawr-O, etc.

3 Dere's a golden slipper in de heavens for you, etc.,
   Before de Lamb of God.

4 I wish I'd been dere when prayer begun, etc.

5 To see my Jesus about my sins, etc.

6 Then home to glory we will go, etc.

[This is interesting as an undoubted variation of "John, John of the holy order." No. 22. A comparison of the words shows that the word "number" should be "member."]

101. THE WINTER.

O de vinter, O de vinter, O de vinter 'll soon be ober,*chilen, De

vinter, O de vinter, O do vinter 'll soon be ober, chilen, De

vinter, O de vinter, O de vinter 'll soon be ober, chilen,

Yes, my Lord! 1. 'Tis Paul and Silas bound in chains, chains, And

one did weep,† and de o - der one did pray, o - der one did pray!

2 You bend your knees ‡ on holy ground, ground,
   And ask de Lord, Lord, for to turn you around.
     For de vinter, etc.

3 I turn my eyes towards the sky, sky,
   And ask de Lord, Lord, for wings to fly.

4 For you see me gwine 'long so, so,
   I has my tri-trials yer below.

Am a-comin'.   † Sing.   ‡ I bend my knees, etc.

102. THE HEAVEN BELLS.

1. O mother I be - li - eve.... O mother I be - li - eve....

O mother I be - li - eve That Christ was cru - ci -

- fied! O don't you hear the Heaven bells a -

- ring - ing o - ver me? a - ring - ing o - ver me? a -

-ringing o - ver me? O don't you hear the Heaven bells a -

- ring - ing o - ver me? It sounds like the judgment day!

III.

INLAND SLAVE STATES:

Including Tennessee, Arkansas, and the Mississippi River.

SLAVE SONGS OF THE UNITED STATES.

III.

103. THE GOLD BAND.

1. Gwine to march a - way in de gold band, In de army, bye-and-bye; Gwine to march a - way in de gold band, In de ar - my, bye-and-bye. Sinner, what you gwine to do dat day? Sinner, what you gwine to do dat day? When de fire's a - roll - ing be - hind you, In de ar - my, bye-and-bye.

2 Sister Mary gwine to hand down the robe,
    In the army, bye-and-bye ;
  Gwine to hand down the robe and the gold band,
    In the army, bye-and-bye.

104. THE GOOD OLD WAY.

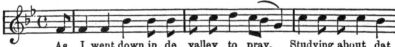

As I went down in de valley to pray, Studying about dat

good old way, When you shall wear de starry crown, Good Lord,

show me de way. O mourner,*let's go down, let's go down,let's go down,

O mourner, let's go down, Down in de valley to pray.

* Sister, etc.

105. I'M GOING HOME.

1. I sought my Lord in de wilderness, in de wilderness, in de

wil-der-ness; I sought my Lord in de wil-der-ness, For

I'm a-go-ing home. For I'm going home, For I'm going

home; I'm just getting read-y, For I'm go-ing home.

2 I found free grace in the wilderness,

3 My father preaches in the wilderness.

106. SINNER WON'T DIE NO MORE.

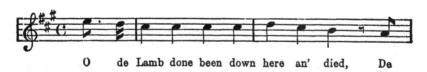

O   de Lamb done been down here an' died,   De

Lamb done been down here an' died, O   de Lamb done been down

here an' died, Sin - ner won't die   no   mo'.   1. I

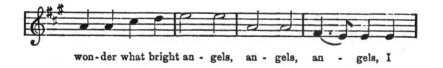

won-der what bright an - gels, an - gels, an - gels, I

wonder what bright an - gels, De robes all   ready   now.

2 O see dem ships come a-sailing, sailing, sailing,

O see dem ships come a-sailing,

De robes all ready now.

107. BROTHER, GUIDE ME HOME.

Brudder, guide me home an' I am glad, Bright

an - gels bid - dy me to come; Brudder, guide me home an'

I am glad, Bright an - gels bid - dy me to come.

1. What a hap - py time, chil'n, What a happy time, chil'n, What a

hap- py time, chil - 'n, Bright an - gels biddy me to come.

2 Let's go to God, chil'n, (*ter*)
Bright angels biddy me to come.

[I heard this in a praise-house at the "Contraband Camp" on President's Island near Memphis, in September, 1864. I will not vouch for the absolute accuracy of my memory.—W. F. A.]

108. LITTLE CHILDREN, THEN WON'T YOU BE GLAD?

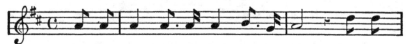

1. Lit - tle   children, then won't you be glad,   Lit - tle

children, then won't you be glad, That you have been to heav'n, an' you're

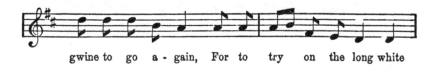

gwine to go   a - gain, For to   try   on   the long white

robe,   children, For   to   try   on   the long white robe.

2 King Jesus, he was so strong (*ter*), my Lord,
   That he jarred down the walls of hell.

3 Don't you hear what de chariot say? (*bis*)
   De fore wheels run by de grace ob God,
   An' de hind wheels dey run by faith.

4 Don't you 'member what you promise de Lord? (*bis*)
   You promise de Lord that you would feed his sheep,
   An' gather his lambs so well.

[Often sung in the colored schools at Helena, Arkansas.]

109. CHARLESTON GALS.

1. As I walked down the new-cut road, I met the tap and

then the toad; The toad commenced to whistle and sing, And the

possum cut the pigeon - wing. A - long come an old man

rid - ing by: Old man, if you don't mind, your horse will die ;

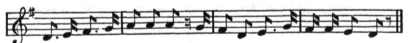

If he dies I'll tan his skin, And if he lives I'll ride him a - gin.

Hi ho, for Charleston gals ! Charleston gals are the gals for me.

2 As I went a-walking down the street,
   Up steps Charleston gals to take a walk with me.
   I kep' a walking and they kep' a talking,
   I danced with a gal with a hole in her stocking.

110. RUN, NIGGER, RUN!

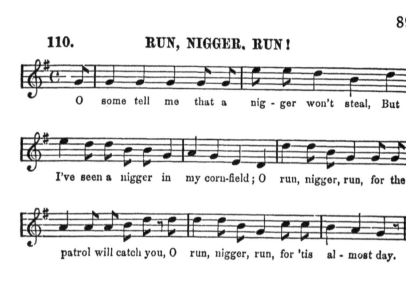

O some tell me that a nig - ger won't steal, But I've seen a nigger in my corn-field; O run, nigger, run, for the patrol will catch you, O run, nigger, run, for 'tis al - most day.

111. I'M GWINE TO ALABAMY.

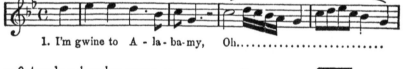

1. I'm gwine to A - la - ba- my, Oh..........................

For to see my mammy, Ah..........................

2 She went from Ole Virginny,—Oh,
   And I'm her pickaninny,—Ah.

3 She lives on the Tombigbee,—Oh,
   I wish I had her wid me,—Ah.

4 Now I'm a good big nigger,—Oh,
   I reckon I won't git bigger,—Ah.

5 But I'd like to see my mammy,—Oh,
   Who lives in Alabamy,—Ah.

[A very good specimen, so far as notes can give one, of the strange barbaric songs that one hears upon the Western steamboats.]

IV.

GULF STATES:

Including Florida and Louisiana: Miscellaneous

SLAVE SONGS OF THE UNITED STATES.

IV.

112. **MY FATHER, HOW LONG?**

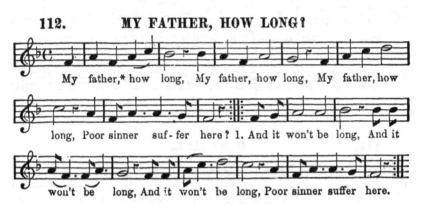

My father,* how long, My father, how long, My father, how long, Poor sinner suf-fer here? 1. And it won't be long, And it won't be long, And it won't be long, Poor sinner suffer here.

2 We'll soon be free, (ter)
  De Lord will call us home.

3 We'll walk de miry road
  Where pleasure never dies.

4 We'll walk de golden streets
  Of de New Jerusalem.

5 My brudders do sing
  De praises of de Lord.

6 We'll fight for liberty
  When de Lord will call us home.

* Mother, etc.

[For singing this "the negroes had been put in jail at Georgetown, S. C., at the outbreak of the Rebellion. 'We'll soon be free' was too dangerous an assertion, and though the chant was an old one, it was no doubt sung with re doubled emphasis during the new events. 'De Lord will call us home,' was evidently thought to be a symbolical verse; for, as a little drummer boy explained it to me, showing all his white teeth as he sat in the moonlight by the door of my tent, 'Dey tink *de Lord* mean for say *de Yankees.*'"—T. W. H.]

113.　　　　**I'M IN TROUBLE.**

I'm in trouble, Lord, I'm in trouble, I'm in trouble, Lord,

| 1st. |　Fine. | 2d.

trouble about my grave, trouble a - bout my grave. Sometimes I

weep, sometimes I mourn, I'm in trouble a - bout my grave; Sometimes I

D.C.

can't do neither one, I'm in trouble a - bout my grave.

114.　　　　**O DANIEL.**

You call yourself church-member, You hold your head so high, You

praise God with your glitt'ring tongue, But you leave all your heart be-

- hind. O my Lord de - li - vered Dan - iel, O

Dan - iel, O Dan - iel, O my Lord de - li - vered

Dan - iel, O why not de - li - ver me too?

115. O BROTHERS, DON'T GET WEARY.

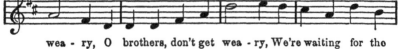

O brothers, don't get wea - ry, O brothers, don't get

wea - ry, O brothers, don't get wea - ry, We're waiting for the

Lord. We'll land on Canaan's shore, We'll land on Canaan's

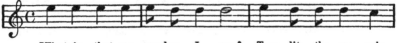

shore, When we land on Canaan's shore, We'll meet forev - er more.

116. I WANT TO JOIN THE BAND.

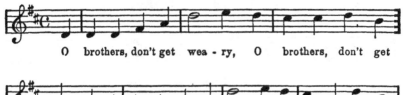

What is that up yonder I see? Two lit - tle an - gels

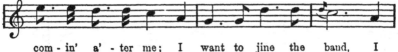

com - in' a' - ter me; I want to jine the band, I

want to jine the band, (Sing togeth - er) I want to jine the band.

117. JACOB'S LADDER.

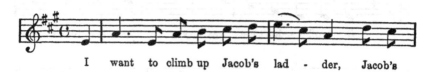

I want to climb up Jacob's lad - der, Jacob's

lad - der, O Jacob's lad - der, I want to climb up Jacob's

lad - der, But I can't climb it till I make my

peace with the Lord. O praise ye the Lord, I'll praise Him till I
O praise the Lord, O praise ye the

die, I'll praise Him till I die, And sing Je - ru - sa - lem,
Lord.

118. PRAY ON.

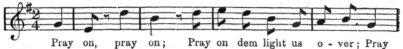

Pray on, pray on; Pray on dem light us o - ver; Pray

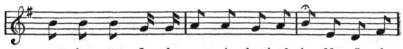

on, Pray on, De u - nion break of day. My sister, you come to

see bap - tize, In de u - nion break of day; My 'loved

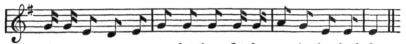

sister, you come to see baptize, In de un - ion break of day.

[As an interpretation of "dem light us over," I suggest "de night is over;" and "union" should probably have a capital *U*. "De night is over; de Union break of day (da comin')." The interchange of *l* and *n* is not uncommon, and is illustrated again in this song in the word "Union," which was pronounced "yuliul" by the person who sung it to me. This song and Nos. 38, 41, 42, 43, 119, 122, and 123, came on to the plantation after I left.—C. P. W.]

119. GOOD NEWS, MEMBER.

Good news, member, good news, member, Don't you mind what Satan say;

Good news, member, good news, And I hearde from heav'n to - day.

1. My brud-der have a seat and I so glad,

Good news, mem - ber, good news; My brudder have a seat and

I so glad, And I hearde from heav'n to - day.

2 Mr. Hawley have a home in Paradise.
3 Archangel bring baptizing down.

120. I WANT TO DIE LIKE-A LAZARUS DIE.

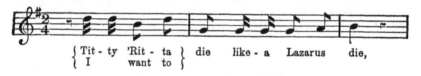

{ Tit - ty 'Rit - ta }
{ I   want to } die like - a Lazarus die,

Die like - a Lazarus die; I want to die like - a Lazarus

die, like - a Lazarus die, like - a Lazarus die.

121. AWAY DOWN IN SUNBURY.

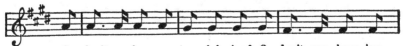

{ O massa take dat new bran coat And hang it on de wall, }
{ Dat darkee take dat same ole coat And wear 'em to de ball. }

O don't you hear my true lub sing? O don't you hear 'em

sigh? A - way down in Sun - bur - y I'm bound to live and die.

122. THIS IS THE TROUBLE OF THE WORLD.

I ax Fa - der Georgy for re - li - gion, Fa - der

Georgy wouldn't give me re - li - gion; You

give me re - li - gion for to run to my el - der; O

dis is de trouble of de world. Dis is de trouble of de

world, O,* Dis is de trouble of de world.

(what you { doubt { for ?)
   { shame }
(take it   ea - sy)
(Tit - ty   'Me - lia)

  * (What you doubt for ?) etc.

123. LEAN ON THE LORD'S SIDE.

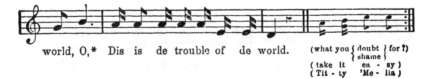

1. Wai', poor Dan - iel, He lean on de Lord's side; (Say)

Dan - iel rock de li - on joy,* Lean on de

Lord's side. 2. (Say) De gold - en chain † to ease him down.

3 De silver spade to dig his grave ;
He lean, etc.

* *i. e.* Daniel (as if Samson) racked the lion's *jaw.* † Band.

A Port Royal variation of " Who is on the Lord's side" (No. 75.)

124. THESE ARE ALL MY FATHER'S CHILDREN.

Dese all my fader's children, Dese all my fader's children,

Dese all my fa - der's children, Out - shine de sun.

My fader's done wid de trouble o' de world, wid de

trouble o' de world, wid de trouble o' de world, My

fader's done wid de trouble o' de world, Outshine de sun.

[This is interesting as being probably the original of "Trouble of the world" (No. 10.) and peculiarly so from the following custom, which is described by a North Carolina negro as existing in South Carolina. When a *pater-familias* dies, his family assemble in the room where the coffin is, and, ranging themselves round the body in the order of age and relationship, sing this hymn, marching round and round. They also take the youngest and pass him first over and then under the coffin. Then two men take the coffin on their shoulders and carry it on the run to the grave.]

125. THE OLD SHIP OF ZION.

[We have received two versions of the "Old Ship of Zion," quite different from each other and from those given by Col. Higginson. The first was sung twenty-five years ago by the colored people of Ann Arundel Co., Maryland. The words may be found in "The Chorus" (Philadelphia: A. S. Jenks, 1860,) p. 170. (Compare, also, p. 167.)

1. What ship is that you're en-list-ed up-on? O glo-ry hal-le-

-lu-jah! 'Tis the old ship of Zi-on, hal-le-

-lu-jah! 'Tis the old ship of Zi-on, hal-le-lu-jah!

2 And who is the Captain of the ship that you're on?—O glory, etc.

My Saviour is the Captain, hallelujah!

[The other is from North Carolina :]

1. Don't you see that ship a-sail-in', a-sail-in', a-

- sail - in', Don't you see that ship a - sail - in', Gwine

o - ver to the Prom - ised Land? I asked my Lord, shall I

ev - er be the one, shall I ev - er be the one, shall I

ev - er be the one, To go sail - in', sail - in',

sail - in', sail - in', Gwine o - ver to the Promised Land?

2 She sails like she is heavy loaded.

3 King Jesus is the Captain.

4 The Holy Ghost is the Pilot.

126. ## COME ALONG, MOSES.

Come a - long, Mo- ses,* don't get lost, don't get lost, don't get lost,

Come a - long, Mo- ses, don't get lost, We are the people† of

God. 1. We have a just God to plead-a our cause, to

plead-a our cause, to plead-a our cause, We have a just God to

plead - a our cause, We are the peo - ple of God.

2 He sits in the Heaven and he answers prayer.

3 Stretch out your rod and come across.

* Judy, Aaron. † Children.

[This air has in parts a suspicious resemblance to the Sunday-school hymn "'Tis religion that can give," which has become very wide-spread in the South since the war. Mrs. James, however, heard it from an old woman in North Carolina, early in 1862, which would seem to vouch for its genuineness.]

127. **THE SOCIAL BAND.**

Bright an-gels on the wa-ter, Hovering by the light; Poor

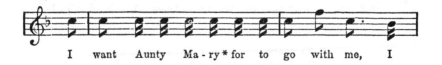

sin-ner stand in the dark ness, And can-not see the light.

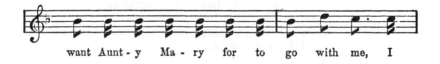

I want Aunty Ma-ry* for to go with me, I

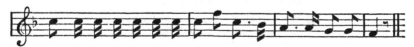

want Aunt-y Ma-ry for to go with me, I

want Aunty Mary for to go with me, To join the social band.

* Brother David.

128.   GOD GOT PLENTY O' ROOM.

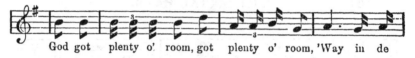

God got   plenty o' room, got   plenty o' room, 'Way in de

kingdom, God got plenty o' room my Je-sus say, 'Way in de

kingdom.   1. Brethren, I   have come a-gain, 'Way in de

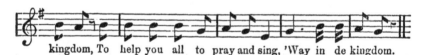

kingdom, To   help you all   to pray and sing, 'Way in de kingdom.

2 So many-a weeks and days have passed
   Since we met together last.

3 Old Satan tremble when he sees
   The weakest saints upon their knees.

4 Prayer makes the darkest cloud withdraw,
   Prayer climbed the ladder Jacob saw.

5 Daniel's wisdom may I know,
   Stephen's faith and spirit sure.

6 John's divine communion feel,
   Joseph's meek and Joshua's zeal.

7 There is a school on earth begun
   Supported by the Holy One.

8 We soon shall lay our school-books by,
   And shout salvation as I fly.

[The above is given exactly as it was sung, some of the measures in ⅜, some in ⅜, and some in ¾ time. The irregularity probably arises from omission of rests, but it seemed a hopeless undertaking to attempt to restore the correct time, and it was thought best to give it in this shape as at any rate a characteristic specimen of negro singing. The song was obtained of a North Carolina negro, who said it came from Virginia.]

129. YOU MUST BE PURE AND HOLY.

1. When I was wick-ed an'-a prone to sin, My

Lord, brether-en, ah my Lord! I thought that I couldn't be

born a - gin, My Lord, breth-er - en, ah my Lord!

CHORUS.

You must be pure and ho - ly, You must be pure an' - a

ho - ly, You must be pure and ho-ly To see God feed his lambs.

2 I'll run all round the cross and cry,
  My Lord, bretheren, ah my Lord,
Or give me Jesus, or I die,
  My Lord, bretheren, ah my Lord.

You must be pure and holy, etc.

3 The Devil am a liar and conjurer too,
    My Lord, etc.   (conjure you,
If you don't look out he'll { cut you in two,
    My Lord, etc.   (cut you through,

4 O run up, sonny, and get your crown,
    My Lord, etc.
And by your Father sit you down,
    My Lord, etc.

5 I was pretty young when I begun,
    My Lord, etc.
But, now my work is almost done,
    My Lord, etc.

6 The Devil's mad and I am glad,
    My Lord, etc.
He lost this soul, he thought he had,
    My Lord, etc.

7 Go 'way, Satan, I don't mind you,
    My Lord, etc.
You wonder, too, that you can't go through,
    My Lord, etc.

8 A lilly * white stone came rolling down,
    My Lord, etc.
It rolled like thunder through the town,
    My Lord, etc.

           * *Qu.* little. ?

[This is a favorite and apparently genuine song which "flourishes" in a colored church at Auburn, N. Y. having been introduced there from the South. "It is sung on *all* occasions, and without any regard to *order* in the verses ; you may not be able to see any connection between any of them. The chorus is always sung once or twice before the verses are used at all. You will see that occasionally there is inserted an extra syllable (ah) and always in the 2nd and 4th lines of the verses ; why this is done I am unable to discover, but it appears to assist them wonderfully in singing. The first note in the chorus is sung very *loud*, and is prolonged to an indefinite time, at the pleasure of the leader. You will notice that the air is in the minor mode, but the chorus, with the exception of the last line, in the major."—W. A. B.]

130. **BELLE LAYOTTE.**

Mo dé - jà rou - lé tout la côte Pan - cor ouar par - eil

belle La - yotte. (*bis*) 1. Mo rou - lé tout la côte,

Mo rou - lé tout la col - o - nie; Mo pan - cor ouar

griffonne la Qua mo gout comme la belle La - yotte.

2 Jean Babet, mon ami,
  Si vous couri par en haut,
  Vous mandé belle Layotte
  Cadeau la li té p. mi mouin.

3 Domestique la maison
  Yé tout faché avec mouin,
  Paraporte chanson la
  Mo composé pou la belle **Layotte.**

131.   **RÉMON.**

SOLO.

Mo par - lé Ré - mon, Ré - mon, Li par - lé Si - mon, Si -
- mon, Li par - lé Ti - tine, Ti - tine, Li tom - bé dans chagrin.

CHORUS.

O femme Rom - u - lus, oh! Belle femme Romu - lus, oh! O
femme Rom - u - lus, oh! Belle femme qui ça vou - lé mo fai.

132.   **AURORE BRADAIRE.**

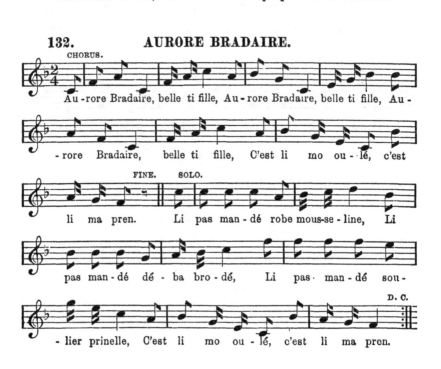

CHORUS.

Au - rore Bradaire, belle ti fille, Au - rore Bradaire, belle ti fille, Au -
- rore Bradaire, belle ti fille, C'est li mo ou - lé, c'est

FINE. SOLO.

li ma pren. Li pas man - dé robe mous-se - line, Li
pas man - dé dé - ba bro - dé, Li pas - man - dé sou -

D. C.

- lier prinelle, C'est li mo ou - lé, c'est li ma pren.

133, **CAROLINE.**

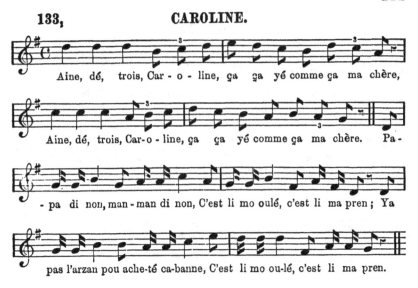

Aine, dé, trois, Car - o - line, ça ça yé comme ça ma chère,

Aine, dé, trois, Car-o - line, ça ça yé comme ça ma chère. Pa-

- pa di non, man - man di non, C'est li mo oulé, c'est li ma pren ; Ya

pas l'arzan pou ache-té ca-banne, C'est li mo ou-lé, c'est li ma pren.

134. **CALINDA.**

SOLO.

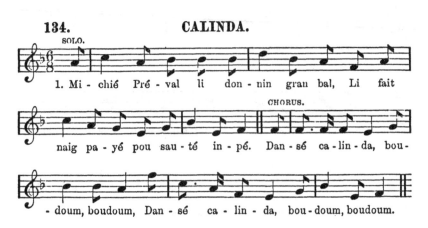

1. Mi - chié Pré - val li don - nin gran bal, Li fait

CHORUS.

naig pa - yé pou sau - té in - pé. Dan - sé ca - lin - da, bou-

- doum, boudoum, Dan - sé ca - lin - da, bou - doum, boudoum.

2 Michié Préval li té capitaine bal,
  So cocher Louis té maite cérémonie.

3 Dans lequirie la yavé gran gala,
  Mo cré choual layé té bien étonné.

4 Yavé des négresse belle passé maitresse,
  Yé volé bébelle dans l'ormoire mamzelle.

135. **LOLOTTE.**

Pauve pi - ti Lolotte a mouin, Pauve pi - ti Lolotte a mouin,

Pauve pi - ti Lolotte a mouin, Li gaignin doulair. Ca - la -

- lou por - té madrasse, li por - té ji - pon gar - ni, Ca - la -

- lou por - té madrasse, li por - té ji - pon gar - ni.

Pauve pi - ti Lolotte a mouin, Pauve pi - ti Lolotte a mouin,

Pauve pi - ti Lo - lotte a mouin, Li gai - gnin

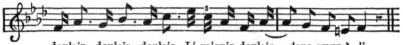

doulair, doulair, doulair, Li gaignin doulair dans cœur à li.

136.   MUSIEU BAINJO.

Voyez   ce mu - let   là,   Musieu Bainjo, Comme il est in - so -

FINE.   D. C.

- lent.   { Chapeau   sur   cô - té,   Musieu Bain - jo,)
          { La canne à   la   main, Musieu Bain - jo, }
          { Botte qui fait crin, crin, Musieu Bain - jo,)

[The seven foregoing songs were obtained from a lady who heard them sung,
before the war, on the "Good Hope" plantation, St. Charles Parish, Louisiana.
The language, evidently a rude corruption of French, is that spoken by the negroes
in that part of the State; and it is said that it is more difficult for persons who
speak French to interpret this dialect, than for those who speak English to understand the most corrupt of the ordinary negro-talk. The pronunciation of this
negro-French is indicated, as accurately as possible, in the versions given here,
which furnish, also, many interesting examples of the peculiar phrases and
idioms employed by this people. The frequent omission of prepositions, articles, and auxiliary verbs, as well as of single letters, and the contractions constantly occurring, are among the most noticeable peculiarities. Some of the
most difficult words are: *mo* for *me, mon, je; li* for *lui, le, la, il, elle; mouin* for
moi; yé for *ils, leur; aine, dé,* for *un, deux; té* for *été, était; ya, yavé* for *il y a,*
etc.; *ouar* for *voir* and its inflections; *oulé* for *vouloir,* etc.; *pancor* for *pas en-
core; michié* for *monsieur; inpé* for *un peu.* The words are, of course, to be
pronounced as if they were pure French.

Four of these songs, Nos. 130, 131, 132 and 133, were sung to a simple dance,
a sort of minuet, called the *Coonjai;* the name and the dance are probably both
of African origin. When the *Coonjai* is danced, the music is furnished by an
orchestra of singers, the leader of whom—a man selected both for the quality of
his voice and for his skill in improvising—sustains the solo part, while the others
afford him an opportunity, as they shout in chorus, for inventing some neat
verse to compliment some lovely *danseuse,* or celebrate the deeds of some plantation hero. The dancers themselves never sing, as in the case of the religious
"shout" of the Port Royal negroes; and the usual musical accompaniment, besides that of the singers, is that furnished by a skilful performer on the barrel-
head-drum, the jaw-bone and key, or some other rude instrument.

No. 134. The "calinda" was a sort of contra-dance, which has now passed
entirely out of use. Bescherelle describes the two lines as "avançant et recu-
lant en cadence, et faisant des contorsions fort singulières et des gestes fort
lascifs."

The first movement of No. 135, "Lolotte," has furnished M. Gottschalk with
the theme of his "Ballade Créole," "La Savane," op. 3 de la Louisiane.

In 136, we have the attempt of some enterprising negro to write a French
song; he is certainly to be congratulated on his success.

It will be noticed that all these songs are "seculars"; and that while the
words of most of them are of very little account, the music is as peculiar, as
interesting, and, in the case of two or three of them, as difficult to write down,
or to sing correctly, as any that have preceded them.]

EDITORS' NOTE.

THE original arrangement of the foregoing collection has not been adhered to. Why the secular songs do not appear by themselves has been already explained. That the division into parts is not strictly geographical was caused by the tardy arrival of most of the songs contained in Part IV. Should a second edition ever be justified by the favor with which the present is received, these irregularities will be corrected.

It was proposed to print music without words, and words without music, each by themselves. But the first can hardly be said to have been obtained, unless "Shock along, John," No. 86, is an instance. The words without music which in one or two cases were kindly, and we fear laboriously, communicated to us, presented no fresh or striking peculiarities, and we therefore decided against their admission.

As was remarked in the Introduction, we are fully aware of the incompleteness of this collection, though we may fairly enough assume it to be *la crême de la crême*. Col. Higginson writes :

"I wish you would look up one 'spiritual,' of which I only remember the chorus—'*It doth appear*'—as being often sung in camp. Also, '*Ring dat charming bell*,' which they used to sing to please Mrs. Saxton, who liked it."

Gen. James H. Wilson, who, in the earlier part of the war, was at Port Royal, and, during explorations and night surveys of the coast between there and Ossabaw Sound, had frequent opportunities of hearing every grade of "spirituals," writes, of Col. Higginson's collection in the *Atlantic Monthly:*

"He has omitted two which I heard more generally sung than any others. I refer to the one beginning :

<blockquote>

"'They took ole Master Lord,
And fed him on pepper and gall,'

</blockquote>

and the other :

<blockquote>

"'My brudder Johnny's new-born baby,
Hi oh, de new-born !'

</blockquote>

"The airs to which these were sung are very peculiar, while the burthen of the songs is pretty clearly indicated by the lines given above. The first seems to allude to the persecutions of Christ, while the latter simply refers to the birth and early death of a new-born baby, and is varied by making a new verse for all the brothers and sisters that the singer happens to be able to call to mind.

"I also recollect the refrain of a boat-song which a crew of ten stalwart negroes used to sing for me in our excursions, but I am inclined to the belief that it was by no means a 'spiritual,' as I could never get any of them to explain it to my satisfaction. The only words I could make out clearly were :

"'Jah de window, jah!
Oh jah de window,' etc.

and the meaning of which I took to be ''jar the window.' If they had any such thing among them, this was probably a fragment of a simple ballad, describing an incident in a negro courtship. I got this impression at the time, partly from the peculiar tone of the song, and partly from their hesitancy to explain it. But whatever may have been its real character, it was quite musical, and had such an inspiring effect upon my boatmen that I have known them to row eighteen or twenty miles, exerting their utmost strength, keeping perfect time to its notes, and never pausing for breath."

These, certainly, are songs to be desired and regretted. But we do not despair of recovering them and others perhaps equally characteristic for a second edition; and we herewith solicit the kind offices of collectors into whose hands this volume may have fallen, in extending and perfecting our researches. For fully a third of the songs recorded by Col. Higginson we have failed to obtain the music, and they may very well serve as a guide for future investigators. We shall also gratefully acknowledge any errors of fact or of typography that may be brought to our attention, and in general anything that would enhance the value or the interest of this collection. Communications may be addressed to Mr. W. P. Garrison, Office of *The Nation* newspaper, New York City.

NOVEMBER, 1867.

A CATALOG OF SELECTED
DOVER BOOKS
IN ALL FIELDS OF INTEREST

A CATALOG OF SELECTED DOVER
BOOKS IN ALL FIELDS OF INTEREST

100 BEST-LOVED POEMS, Edited by Philip Smith. "The Passionate Shepherd to His Love," "Shall I compare thee to a summer's day?" "Death, be not proud," "The Raven," "The Road Not Taken," plus works by Blake, Wordsworth, Byron, Shelley, Keats, many others. 96pp. 5³⁄₁₆ x 8¼. 0-486-28553-7

100 SMALL HOUSES OF THE THIRTIES, Brown-Blodgett Company. Exterior photographs and floor plans for 100 charming structures. Illustrations of models accompanied by descriptions of interiors, color schemes, closet space, and other amenities. 200 illustrations. 112pp. 8⅜ x 11. 0-486-44131-8

1000 TURN-OF-THE-CENTURY HOUSES: With Illustrations and Floor Plans, Herbert C. Chivers. Reproduced from a rare edition, this showcase of homes ranges from cottages and bungalows to sprawling mansions. Each house is meticulously illustrated and accompanied by complete floor plans. 256pp. 9⅜ x 12¼.
0-486-45596-3

101 GREAT AMERICAN POEMS, Edited by The American Poetry & Literacy Project. Rich treasury of verse from the 19th and 20th centuries includes works by Edgar Allan Poe, Robert Frost, Walt Whitman, Langston Hughes, Emily Dickinson, T. S. Eliot, other notables. 96pp. 5³⁄₁₆ x 8¼. 0-486-40158-8

101 GREAT SAMURAI PRINTS, Utagawa Kuniyoshi. Kuniyoshi was a master of the warrior woodblock print — and these 18th-century illustrations represent the pinnacle of his craft. Full-color portraits of renowned Japanese samurais pulse with movement, passion, and remarkably fine detail. 112pp. 8⅜ x 11. 0-486-46523-3

ABC OF BALLET, Janet Grosser. Clearly worded, abundantly illustrated little guide defines basic ballet-related terms: arabesque, battement, pas de chat, relevé, sissonne, many others. Pronunciation guide included. Excellent primer. 48pp. 4³⁄₁₆ x 5¾.
0-486-40871-X

ACCESSORIES OF DRESS: An Illustrated Encyclopedia, Katherine Lester and Bess Viola Oerke. Illustrations of hats, veils, wigs, cravats, shawls, shoes, gloves, and other accessories enhance an engaging commentary that reveals the humor and charm of the many-sided story of accessorized apparel. 644 figures and 59 plates. 608pp. 6⅛ x 9¼.
0-486-43378-1

ADVENTURES OF HUCKLEBERRY FINN, Mark Twain. Join Huck and Jim as their boyhood adventures along the Mississippi River lead them into a world of excitement, danger, and self-discovery. Humorous narrative, lyrical descriptions of the Mississippi valley, and memorable characters. 224pp. 5³⁄₁₆ x 8¼. 0-486-28061-6

ALICE STARMORE'S BOOK OF FAIR ISLE KNITTING, Alice Starmore. A noted designer from the region of Scotland's Fair Isle explores the history and techniques of this distinctive, stranded-color knitting style and provides copious illustrated instructions for 14 original knitwear designs. 208pp. 8⅜ x 10⅞. 0-486-47218-3

Browse over 9,000 books at www.doverpublications.com

ALICE'S ADVENTURES IN WONDERLAND, Lewis Carroll. Beloved classic about a little girl lost in a topsy-turvy land and her encounters with the White Rabbit, March Hare, Mad Hatter, Cheshire Cat, and other delightfully improbable characters. 42 illustrations by Sir John Tenniel. 96pp. 5³⁄₁₆ x 8¼.   0-486-27543-4

AMERICA'S LIGHTHOUSES: An Illustrated History, Francis Ross Holland. Profusely illustrated fact-filled survey of American lighthouses since 1716. Over 200 stations — East, Gulf, and West coasts, Great Lakes, Hawaii, Alaska, Puerto Rico, the Virgin Islands, and the Mississippi and St. Lawrence Rivers. 240pp. 8 x 10¾.
0-486-25576-X

AN ENCYCLOPEDIA OF THE VIOLIN, Alberto Bachmann. Translated by Frederick H. Martens. Introduction by Eugene Ysaye. First published in 1925, this renowned reference remains unsurpassed as a source of essential information, from construction and evolution to repertoire and technique. Includes a glossary and 73 illustrations. 496pp. 6½ x 9¼.   0-486-46618-3

ANIMALS: 1,419 Copyright-Free Illustrations of Mammals, Birds, Fish, Insects, etc., Selected by Jim Harter. Selected for its visual impact and ease of use, this outstanding collection of wood engravings presents over 1,000 species of animals in extremely lifelike poses. Includes mammals, birds, reptiles, amphibians, fish, insects, and other invertebrates. 284pp. 9 x 12.   0-486-23766-4

THE ANNALS, Tacitus. Translated by Alfred John Church and William Jackson Brodribb. This vital chronicle of Imperial Rome, written by the era's great historian, spans A.D. 14-68 and paints incisive psychological portraits of major figures, from Tiberius to Nero. 416pp. 5³⁄₁₆ x 8¼.   0-486-45236-0

ANTIGONE, Sophocles. Filled with passionate speeches and sensitive probing of moral and philosophical issues, this powerful and often-performed Greek drama reveals the grim fate that befalls the children of Oedipus. Footnotes. 64pp. 5³⁄₁₆ x 8 ¼.   0-486-27804-2

ART DECO DECORATIVE PATTERNS IN FULL COLOR, Christian Stoll. Reprinted from a rare 1910 portfolio, 160 sensuous and exotic images depict a breathtaking array of florals, geometrics, and abstracts — all elegant in their stark simplicity. 64pp. 8⅜ x 11.   0-486-44862-2

THE ARTHUR RACKHAM TREASURY: 86 Full-Color Illustrations, Arthur Rackham. Selected and Edited by Jeff A. Menges. A stunning treasury of 86 full-page plates span the famed English artist's career, from *Rip Van Winkle* (1905) to masterworks such as *Undine, A Midsummer Night's Dream,* and *Wind in the Willows* (1939). 96pp. 8⅜ x 11.
0-486-44685-9

THE AUTHENTIC GILBERT & SULLIVAN SONGBOOK, W. S. Gilbert and A. S. Sullivan. The most comprehensive collection available, this songbook includes selections from every one of Gilbert and Sullivan's light operas. Ninety-two numbers are presented uncut and unedited, and in their original keys. 410pp. 9 x 12.
0-486-23482-7

THE AWAKENING, Kate Chopin. First published in 1899, this controversial novel of a New Orleans wife's search for love outside a stifling marriage shocked readers. Today, it remains a first-rate narrative with superb characterization. New introductory Note. 128pp. 5³⁄₁₆ x 8¼.   0-486-27786-0

BASIC DRAWING, Louis Priscilla. Beginning with perspective, this commonsense manual progresses to the figure in movement, light and shade, anatomy, drapery, composition, trees and landscape, and outdoor sketching. Black-and-white illustrations throughout. 128pp. 8⅜ x 11.   0-486-45815-6

Browse over 9,000 books at www.doverpublications.com

THE BATTLES THAT CHANGED HISTORY, Fletcher Pratt. Historian profiles 16 crucial conflicts, ancient to modern, that changed the course of Western civilization. Gripping accounts of battles led by Alexander the Great, Joan of Arc, Ulysses S. Grant, other commanders. 27 maps. 352pp. 5⅜ x 8½. 0-486-41129-X

BEETHOVEN'S LETTERS, Ludwig van Beethoven. Edited by Dr. A. C. Kalischer. Features 457 letters to fellow musicians, friends, greats, patrons, and literary men. Reveals musical thoughts, quirks of personality, insights, and daily events. Includes 15 plates. 410pp. 5⅜ x 8½. 0-486-22769-3

BERNICE BOBS HER HAIR AND OTHER STORIES, F. Scott Fitzgerald. This brilliant anthology includes 6 of Fitzgerald's most popular stories: "The Diamond as Big as the Ritz," the title tale, "The Offshore Pirate," "The Ice Palace," "The Jelly Bean," and "May Day." 176pp. 5⅜ x 8½. 0-486-47049-0

BESLER'S BOOK OF FLOWERS AND PLANTS: 73 Full-Color Plates from Hortus Eystettensis, 1613, Basilius Besler. Here is a selection of magnificent plates from the *Hortus Eystettensis*, which vividly illustrated and identified the plants, flowers, and trees that thrived in the legendary German garden at Eichstätt. 80pp. 8⅜ x 11. 0-486-46005-3

THE BOOK OF KELLS, Edited by Blanche Cirker. Painstakingly reproduced from a rare facsimile edition, this volume contains full-page decorations, portraits, illustrations, plus a sampling of textual leaves with exquisite calligraphy and ornamentation. 32 full-color illustrations. 32pp. 9⅜ x 12¼. 0-486-24345-1

THE BOOK OF THE CROSSBOW: With an Additional Section on Catapults and Other Siege Engines, Ralph Payne-Gallwey. Fascinating study traces history and use of crossbow as military and sporting weapon, from Middle Ages to modern times. Also covers related weapons: balistas, catapults, Turkish bows, more. Over 240 illustrations. 400pp. 7¼ x 10⅛. 0-486-28720-3

THE BUNGALOW BOOK: Floor Plans and Photos of 112 Houses, 1910, Henry L. Wilson. Here are 112 of the most popular and economic blueprints of the early 20th century — plus an illustration or photograph of each completed house. A wonderful time capsule that still offers a wealth of valuable insights. 160pp. 8⅜ x 11. 0-486-45104-6

THE CALL OF THE WILD, Jack London. A classic novel of adventure, drawn from London's own experiences as a Klondike adventurer, relating the story of a heroic dog caught in the brutal life of the Alaska Gold Rush. Note. 64pp. 5³⁄₁₆ x 8¼. 0-486-26472-6

CANDIDE, Voltaire. Edited by Francois-Marie Arouet. One of the world's great satires since its first publication in 1759. Witty, caustic skewering of romance, science, philosophy, religion, government — nearly all human ideals and institutions. 112pp. 5³⁄₁₆ x 8¼. 0-486-26689-3

CELEBRATED IN THEIR TIME: Photographic Portraits from the George Grantham Bain Collection, Edited by Amy Pastan. With an Introduction by Michael Carlebach. Remarkable portrait gallery features 112 rare images of Albert Einstein, Charlie Chaplin, the Wright Brothers, Henry Ford, and other luminaries from the worlds of politics, art, entertainment, and industry. 128pp. 8⅜ x 11. 0-486-46754-6

CHARIOTS FOR APOLLO: The NASA History of Manned Lunar Spacecraft to 1969, Courtney G. Brooks, James M. Grimwood, and Loyd S. Swenson, Jr. This illustrated history by a trio of experts is the definitive reference on the Apollo spacecraft and lunar modules. It traces the vehicles' design, development, and operation in space. More than 100 photographs and illustrations. 576pp. 6¾ x 9¼. 0-486-46756-2

A CHRISTMAS CAROL, Charles Dickens. This engrossing tale relates Ebenezer Scrooge's ghostly journeys through Christmases past, present, and future and his ultimate transformation from a harsh and grasping old miser to a charitable and compassionate human being. 80pp. 5³⁄₁₆ x 8¼. 0-486-26865-9

COMMON SENSE, Thomas Paine. First published in January of 1776, this highly influential landmark document clearly and persuasively argued for American separation from Great Britain and paved the way for the Declaration of Independence. 64pp. 5³⁄₁₆ x 8¼. 0-486-29602-4

THE COMPLETE SHORT STORIES OF OSCAR WILDE, Oscar Wilde. Complete texts of "The Happy Prince and Other Tales," "A House of Pomegranates," "Lord Arthur Savile's Crime and Other Stories," "Poems in Prose," and "The Portrait of Mr. W. H." 208pp. 5³⁄₁₆ x 8¼. 0-486-45216-6

COMPLETE SONNETS, William Shakespeare. Over 150 exquisite poems deal with love, friendship, the tyranny of time, beauty's evanescence, death, and other themes in language of remarkable power, precision, and beauty. Glossary of archaic terms. 80pp. 5³⁄₁₆ x 8¼. 0-486-26686-9

THE COUNT OF MONTE CRISTO: Abridged Edition, Alexandre Dumas. Falsely accused of treason, Edmond Dantès is imprisoned in the bleak Chateau d'If. After a hair-raising escape, he launches an elaborate plot to extract a bitter revenge against those who betrayed him. 448pp. 5³⁄₁₆ x 8¼. 0-486-45643-9

CRAFTSMAN BUNGALOWS: Designs from the Pacific Northwest, Yoho & Merritt. This reprint of a rare catalog, showcasing the charming simplicity and cozy style of Craftsman bungalows, is filled with photos of completed homes, plus floor plans and estimated costs. An indispensable resource for architects, historians, and illustrators. 112pp. 10 x 7. 0-486-46875-5

CRAFTSMAN BUNGALOWS: 59 Homes from "The Craftsman," Edited by Gustav Stickley. Best and most attractive designs from Arts and Crafts Movement publication — 1903–1916 — includes sketches, photographs of homes, floor plans, descriptive text. 128pp. 8¼ x 11. 0-486-25829-7

CRIME AND PUNISHMENT, Fyodor Dostoyevsky. Translated by Constance Garnett. Supreme masterpiece tells the story of Raskolnikov, a student tormented by his own thoughts after he murders an old woman. Overwhelmed by guilt and terror, he confesses and goes to prison. 480pp. 5³⁄₁₆ x 8¼. 0-486-41587-2

THE DECLARATION OF INDEPENDENCE AND OTHER GREAT DOCUMENTS OF AMERICAN HISTORY: 1775-1865, Edited by John Grafton. Thirteen compelling and influential documents: Henry's "Give Me Liberty or Give Me Death," Declaration of Independence, The Constitution, Washington's First Inaugural Address, The Monroe Doctrine, The Emancipation Proclamation, Gettysburg Address, more. 64pp. 5³⁄₁₆ x 8¼. 0-486-41124-9

THE DESERT AND THE SOWN: Travels in Palestine and Syria, Gertrude Bell. "The female Lawrence of Arabia," Gertrude Bell wrote captivating, perceptive accounts of her travels in the Middle East. This intriguing narrative, accompanied by 160 photos, traces her 1905 sojourn in Lebanon, Syria, and Palestine. 368pp. 5⅜ x 8½. 0-486-46876-3

A DOLL'S HOUSE, Henrik Ibsen. Ibsen's best-known play displays his genius for realistic prose drama. An expression of women's rights, the play climaxes when the central character, Nora, rejects a smothering marriage and life in "a doll's house." 80pp. 5³⁄₁₆ x 8¼. 0-486-27062-9

DOOMED SHIPS: Great Ocean Liner Disasters, William H. Miller, Jr. Nearly 200 photographs, many from private collections, highlight tales of some of the vessels whose pleasure cruises ended in catastrophe: the *Morro Castle, Normandie, Andrea Doria, Europa,* and many others. 128pp. 8⅜ x 11¼. 0-486-45366-9

THE DORÉ BIBLE ILLUSTRATIONS, Gustave Doré. Detailed plates from the Bible: the Creation scenes, Adam and Eve, horrifying visions of the Flood, the battle sequences with their monumental crowds, depictions of the life of Jesus, 241 plates in all. 241pp. 9 x 12. 0-486-23004-X

DRAWING DRAPERY FROM HEAD TO TOE, Cliff Young. Expert guidance on how to draw shirts, pants, skirts, gloves, hats, and coats on the human figure, including folds in relation to the body, pull and crush, action folds, creases, more. Over 200 drawings. 48pp. 8¼ x 11. 0-486-45591-2

DUBLINERS, James Joyce. A fine and accessible introduction to the work of one of the 20th century's most influential writers, this collection features 15 tales, including a masterpiece of the short-story genre, "The Dead." 160pp. 5³⁄₁₆ x 8¼. 0-486-26870-5

EASY-TO-MAKE POP-UPS, Joan Irvine. Illustrated by Barbara Reid. Dozens of wonderful ideas for three-dimensional paper fun — from holiday greeting cards with moving parts to a pop-up menagerie. Easy-to-follow, illustrated instructions for more than 30 projects. 299 black-and-white illustrations. 96pp. 8⅜ x 11. 0-486-44622-0

EASY-TO-MAKE STORYBOOK DOLLS: A "Novel" Approach to Cloth Dollmaking, Sherralyn St. Clair. Favorite fictional characters come alive in this unique beginner's dollmaking guide. Includes patterns for Pollyanna, Dorothy from *The Wonderful Wizard of Oz,* Mary of *The Secret Garden,* plus easy-to-follow instructions, 263 black-and-white illustrations, and an 8-page color insert. 112pp. 8¼ x 11. 0-486-47360-0

EINSTEIN'S ESSAYS IN SCIENCE, Albert Einstein. Speeches and essays in accessible, everyday language profile influential physicists such as Niels Bohr and Isaac Newton. They also explore areas of physics to which the author made major contributions. 128pp. 5 x 8. 0-486-47011-3

EL DORADO: Further Adventures of the Scarlet Pimpernel, Baroness Orczy. A popular sequel to *The Scarlet Pimpernel,* this suspenseful story recounts the Pimpernel's attempts to rescue the Dauphin from imprisonment during the French Revolution. An irresistible blend of intrigue, period detail, and vibrant characterizations. 352pp. 5³⁄₁₆ x 8¼. 0-486-44026-5

ELEGANT SMALL HOMES OF THE TWENTIES: 99 Designs from a Competition, Chicago Tribune. Nearly 100 designs for five- and six-room houses feature New England and Southern colonials, Normandy cottages, stately Italianate dwellings, and other fascinating snapshots of American domestic architecture of the 1920s. 112pp. 9 x 12. 0-486-46910-7

THE ELEMENTS OF STYLE: The Original Edition, William Strunk, Jr. This is the book that generations of writers have relied upon for timeless advice on grammar, diction, syntax, and other essentials. In concise terms, it identifies the principal requirements of proper style and common errors. 64pp. 5⅜ x 8¼. 0-486-44798-7

THE ELUSIVE PIMPERNEL, Baroness Orczy. Robespierre's revolutionaries find their wicked schemes thwarted by the heroic Pimpernel — Sir Percival Blakeney. In this thrilling sequel, Chauvelin devises a plot to eliminate the Pimpernel and his wife. 272pp. 5³⁄₁₆ x 8¼. 0-486-45464-9

AN ENCYCLOPEDIA OF BATTLES: Accounts of Over 1,560 Battles from 1479 B.C. to the Present, David Eggenberger. Essential details of every major battle in recorded history from the first battle of Megiddo in 1479 B.C. to Grenada in 1984. List of battle maps. 99 illustrations. 544pp. 6½ x 9¼. 0-486-24913-1

ENCYCLOPEDIA OF EMBROIDERY STITCHES, INCLUDING CREWEL, Marion Nichols. Precise explanations and instructions, clearly illustrated, on how to work chain, back, cross, knotted, woven stitches, and many more — 178 in all, including Cable Outline, Whipped Satin, and Eyelet Buttonhole. Over 1400 illustrations. 219pp. 8⅜ x 11¼. 0-486-22929-7

ENTER JEEVES: 15 Early Stories, P. G. Wodehouse. Splendid collection contains first 8 stories featuring Bertie Wooster, the deliciously dim aristocrat and Jeeves, his brainy, imperturbable manservant. Also, the complete Reggie Pepper (Bertie's prototype) series. 288pp. 5⅜ x 8½. 0-486-29717-9

ERIC SLOANE'S AMERICA: Paintings in Oil, Michael Wigley. With a Foreword by Mimi Sloane. Eric Sloane's evocative oils of America's landscape and material culture shimmer with immense historical and nostalgic appeal. This original hardcover collection gathers nearly a hundred of his finest paintings, with subjects ranging from New England to the American Southwest. 128pp. 10⅝ x 9. 0-486-46525-X

ETHAN FROME, Edith Wharton. Classic story of wasted lives, set against a bleak New England background. Superbly delineated characters in a hauntingly grim tale of thwarted love. Considered by many to be Wharton's masterpiece. 96pp. 5³⁄₁₆ x 8 ¼. 0-486-26690-7

THE EVERLASTING MAN, G. K. Chesterton. Chesterton's view of Christianity — as a blend of philosophy and mythology, satisfying intellect and spirit — applies to his brilliant book, which appeals to readers' heads as well as their hearts. 288pp. 5⅜ x 8½. 0-486-46036-3

THE FIELD AND FOREST HANDY BOOK, Daniel Beard. Written by a co-founder of the Boy Scouts, this appealing guide offers illustrated instructions for building kites, birdhouses, boats, igloos, and other fun projects, plus numerous helpful tips for campers. 448pp. 5³⁄₁₆ x 8¼. 0-486-46191-2

FINDING YOUR WAY WITHOUT MAP OR COMPASS, Harold Gatty. Useful, instructive manual shows would-be explorers, hikers, bikers, scouts, sailors, and survivalists how to find their way outdoors by observing animals, weather patterns, shifting sands, and other elements of nature. 288pp. 5⅜ x 8½. 0-486-40613-X

FIRST FRENCH READER: A Beginner's Dual-Language Book, Edited and Translated by Stanley Appelbaum. This anthology introduces 50 legendary writers — Voltaire, Balzac, Baudelaire, Proust, more — through passages from *The Red and the Black, Les Misérables, Madame Bovary,* and other classics. Original French text plus English translation on facing pages. 240pp. 5⅜ x 8½. 0-486-46178-5

FIRST GERMAN READER: A Beginner's Dual-Language Book, Edited by Harry Steinhauer. Specially chosen for their power to evoke German life and culture, these short, simple readings include poems, stories, essays, and anecdotes by Goethe, Hesse, Heine, Schiller, and others. 224pp. 5⅜ x 8½. 0-486-46179-3

FIRST SPANISH READER: A Beginner's Dual-Language Book, Angel Flores. Delightful stories, other material based on works of Don Juan Manuel, Luis Taboada, Ricardo Palma, other noted writers. Complete faithful English translations on facing pages. Exercises. 176pp. 5⅜ x 8½. 0-486-25810-6

FIVE ACRES AND INDEPENDENCE, Maurice G. Kains. Great back-to-the-land classic explains basics of self-sufficient farming. The one book to get. 95 illustrations. 397pp. 5⅜ x 8½. 0-486-20974-1

FLAGG'S SMALL HOUSES: Their Economic Design and Construction, 1922, Ernest Flagg. Although most famous for his skyscrapers, Flagg was also a proponent of the well-designed single-family dwelling. His classic treatise features innovations that save space, materials, and cost. 526 illustrations. 160pp. 9⅜ x 12¼. 0-486-45197-6

FLATLAND: A Romance of Many Dimensions, Edwin A. Abbott. Classic of science (and mathematical) fiction — charmingly illustrated by the author — describes the adventures of A. Square, a resident of Flatland, in Spaceland (three dimensions), Lineland (one dimension), and Pointland (no dimensions). 96pp. 5³⁄₁₆ x 8¼. 0-486-27263-X

FRANKENSTEIN, Mary Shelley. The story of Victor Frankenstein's monstrous creation and the havoc it caused has enthralled generations of readers and inspired countless writers of horror and suspense. With the author's own 1831 introduction. 176pp. 5³⁄₁₆ x 8¼. 0-486-28211-2

THE GARGOYLE BOOK: 572 Examples from Gothic Architecture, Lester Burbank Bridaham. Dispelling the conventional wisdom that French Gothic architectural flourishes were born of despair or gloom, Bridaham reveals the whimsical nature of these creations and the ingenious artisans who made them. 572 illustrations. 224pp. 8⅜ x 11. 0-486-44754-5

THE GIFT OF THE MAGI AND OTHER SHORT STORIES, O. Henry. Sixteen captivating stories by one of America's most popular storytellers. Included are such classics as "The Gift of the Magi," "The Last Leaf," and "The Ransom of Red Chief." Publisher's Note. 96pp. 5³⁄₁₆ x 8¼. 0-486-27061-0

THE GOETHE TREASURY: Selected Prose and Poetry, Johann Wolfgang von Goethe. Edited, Selected, and with an Introduction by Thomas Mann. In addition to his lyric poetry, Goethe wrote travel sketches, autobiographical studies, essays, letters, and proverbs in rhyme and prose. This collection presents outstanding examples from each genre. 368pp. 5⅜ x 8½. 0-486-44780-4

GREAT EXPECTATIONS, Charles Dickens. Orphaned Pip is apprenticed to the dirty work of the forge but dreams of becoming a gentleman — and one day finds himself in possession of "great expectations." Dickens' finest novel. 400pp. 5³⁄₁₆ x 8¼. 0-486-41586-4

GREAT WRITERS ON THE ART OF FICTION: From Mark Twain to Joyce Carol Oates, Edited by James Daley. An indispensable source of advice and inspiration, this anthology features essays by Henry James, Kate Chopin, Willa Cather, Sinclair Lewis, Jack London, Raymond Chandler, Raymond Carver, Eudora Welty, and Kurt Vonnegut, Jr. 192pp. 5⅜ x 8½. 0-486-45128-3

HAMLET, William Shakespeare. The quintessential Shakespearean tragedy, whose highly charged confrontations and anguished soliloquies probe depths of human feeling rarely sounded in any art. Reprinted from an authoritative British edition complete with illuminating footnotes. 128pp. 5³⁄₁₆ x 8¼. 0-486-27278-8

THE HAUNTED HOUSE, Charles Dickens. A Yuletide gathering in an eerie country retreat provides the backdrop for Dickens and his friends — including Elizabeth Gaskell and Wilkie Collins — who take turns spinning supernatural yarns. 144pp. 5⅜ x 8½. 0-486-46309-5

Browse over 9,000 books at www.doverpublications.com

HEART OF DARKNESS, Joseph Conrad. Dark allegory of a journey up the Congo River and the narrator's encounter with the mysterious Mr. Kurtz. Masterly blend of adventure, character study, psychological penetration. For many, Conrad's finest, most enigmatic story. 80pp. 5³⁄₁₆ x 8¼. 0-486-26464-5

HENSON AT THE NORTH POLE, Matthew A. Henson. This thrilling memoir by the heroic African-American who was Peary's companion through two decades of Arctic exploration recounts a tale of danger, courage, and determination. "Fascinating and exciting." — *Commonweal.* 128pp. 5⅜ x 8½. 0-486-45472-X

HISTORIC COSTUMES AND HOW TO MAKE THEM, Mary Fernald and E. Shenton. Practical, informative guidebook shows how to create everything from short tunics worn by Saxon men in the fifth century to a lady's bustle dress of the late 1800s. 81 illustrations. 176pp. 5⅜ x 8½. 0-486-44906-8

THE HOUND OF THE BASKERVILLES, Arthur Conan Doyle. A deadly curse in the form of a legendary ferocious beast continues to claim its victims from the Baskerville family until Holmes and Watson intervene. Often called the best detective story ever written. 128pp. 5³⁄₁₆ x 8¼. 0-486-28214-7

THE HOUSE BEHIND THE CEDARS, Charles W. Chesnutt. Originally published in 1900, this groundbreaking novel by a distinguished African-American author recounts the drama of a brother and sister who "pass for white" during the dangerous days of Reconstruction. 208pp. 5⅜ x 8½. 0-486-46144-0

THE HUMAN FIGURE IN MOTION, Eadweard Muybridge. The 4,789 photographs in this definitive selection show the human figure — models almost all undraped — engaged in over 160 different types of action: running, climbing stairs, etc. 390pp. 7⅞ x 10⅝. 0-486-20204-6

THE IMPORTANCE OF BEING EARNEST, Oscar Wilde. Wilde's witty and buoyant comedy of manners, filled with some of literature's most famous epigrams, reprinted from an authoritative British edition. Considered Wilde's most perfect work. 64pp. 5³⁄₁₆ x 8¼. 0-486-26478-5

THE INFERNO, Dante Alighieri. Translated and with notes by Henry Wadsworth Longfellow. The first stop on Dante's famous journey from Hell to Purgatory to Paradise, this 14th-century allegorical poem blends vivid and shocking imagery with graceful lyricism. Translated by the beloved 19th-century poet, Henry Wadsworth Longfellow. 256pp. 5³⁄₁₆ x 8¼. 0-486-44288-8

JANE EYRE, Charlotte Brontë. Written in 1847, *Jane Eyre* tells the tale of an orphan girl's progress from the custody of cruel relatives to an oppressive boarding school and its culmination in a troubled career as a governess. 448pp. 5³⁄₁₆ x 8¼.
0-486-42449-9

JAPANESE WOODBLOCK FLOWER PRINTS, Tanigami Kônan. Extraordinary collection of Japanese woodblock prints by a well-known artist features 120 plates in brilliant color. Realistic images from a rare edition include daffodils, tulips, and other familiar and unusual flowers. 128pp. 11 x 8¼. 0-486-46442-3

JEWELRY MAKING AND DESIGN, Augustus F. Rose and Antonio Cirino. Professional secrets of jewelry making are revealed in a thorough, practical guide. Over 200 illustrations. 306pp. 5⅜ x 8½. 0-486-21750-7

JULIUS CAESAR, William Shakespeare. Great tragedy based on Plutarch's account of the lives of Brutus, Julius Caesar and Mark Antony. Evil plotting, ringing oratory, high tragedy with Shakespeare's incomparable insight, dramatic power. Explanatory footnotes. 96pp. 5³⁄₁₆ x 8¼. 0-486-26876-4

THE JUNGLE, Upton Sinclair. 1906 bestseller shockingly reveals intolerable labor practices and working conditions in the Chicago stockyards as it tells the grim story of a Slavic family that emigrates to America full of optimism but soon faces despair. 320pp. 5³⁄₁₆ x 8¼. 0-486-41923-1

THE KINGDOM OF GOD IS WITHIN YOU, Leo Tolstoy. The soul-searching book that inspired Gandhi to embrace the concept of passive resistance, Tolstoy's 1894 polemic clearly outlines a radical, well-reasoned revision of traditional Christian thinking. 352pp. 5³⁄₁₆ x 8¼. 0-486-45138-0

THE LADY OR THE TIGER?: and Other Logic Puzzles, Raymond M. Smullyan. Created by a renowned puzzle master, these whimsically themed challenges involve paradoxes about probability, time, and change; metapuzzles; and self-referentiality. Nineteen chapters advance in difficulty from relatively simple to highly complex. 1982 edition. 240pp. 5⅜ x 8½. 0-486-47027-X

LEAVES OF GRASS: The Original 1855 Edition, Walt Whitman. Whitman's immortal collection includes some of the greatest poems of modern times, including his masterpiece, "Song of Myself." Shattering standard conventions, it stands as an unabashed celebration of body and nature. 128pp. 5³⁄₁₆ x 8¼. 0-486-45676-5

LES MISÉRABLES, Victor Hugo. Translated by Charles E. Wilbour. Abridged by James K. Robinson. A convict's heroic struggle for justice and redemption plays out against a fiery backdrop of the Napoleonic wars. This edition features the excellent original translation and a sensitive abridgment. 304pp. 6⅛ x 9¼. 0-486-45789-3

LILITH: A Romance, George MacDonald. In this novel by the father of fantasy literature, a man travels through time to meet Adam and Eve and to explore humanity's fall from grace and ultimate redemption. 240pp. 5⅜ x 8½. 0-486-46818-6

THE LOST LANGUAGE OF SYMBOLISM, Harold Bayley. This remarkable book reveals the hidden meaning behind familiar images and words, from the origins of Santa Claus to the fleur-de-lys, drawing from mythology, folklore, religious texts, and fairy tales. 1,418 illustrations. 784pp. 5⅜ x 8½. 0-486-44787-1

MACBETH, William Shakespeare. A Scottish nobleman murders the king in order to succeed to the throne. Tortured by his conscience and fearful of discovery, he becomes tangled in a web of treachery and deceit that ultimately spells his doom. 96pp. 5³⁄₁₆ x 8¼. 0-486-27802-6

MAKING AUTHENTIC CRAFTSMAN FURNITURE: Instructions and Plans for 62 Projects, Gustav Stickley. Make authentic reproductions of handsome, functional, durable furniture: tables, chairs, wall cabinets, desks, a hall tree, and more. Construction plans with drawings, schematics, dimensions, and lumber specs reprinted from 1900s The Craftsman magazine. 128pp. 8⅛ x 11. 0-486-25000-8

MATHEMATICS FOR THE NONMATHEMATICIAN, Morris Kline. Erudite and entertaining overview follows development of mathematics from ancient Greeks to present. Topics include logic and mathematics, the fundamental concept, differential calculus, probability theory, much more. Exercises and problems. 641pp. 5⅜ x 8½. 0-486-24823-2

MEMOIRS OF AN ARABIAN PRINCESS FROM ZANZIBAR, Emily Ruete. This 19th-century autobiography offers a rare inside look at the society surrounding a sultan's palace. A real-life princess in exile recalls her vanished world of harems, slave trading, and court intrigues. 288pp. 5⅜ x 8½. 0-486-47121-7

Browse over 9,000 books at www.doverpublications.com

THE METAMORPHOSIS AND OTHER STORIES, Franz Kafka. Excellent new English translations of title story (considered by many critics Kafka's most perfect work), plus "The Judgment," "In the Penal Colony," "A Country Doctor," and "A Report to an Academy." Note. 96pp. 5$\frac{3}{16}$ x 8$\frac{1}{4}$. 0-486-29030-1

MICROSCOPIC ART FORMS FROM THE PLANT WORLD, R. Anheisser. From undulating curves to complex geometrics, a world of fascinating images abound in this classic, illustrated survey of microscopic plants. Features 400 detailed illustrations of nature's minute but magnificent handiwork. The accompanying CD-ROM includes all of the images in the book. 128pp. 9 x 9. 0-486-46013-4

A MIDSUMMER NIGHT'S DREAM, William Shakespeare. Among the most popular of Shakespeare's comedies, this enchanting play humorously celebrates the vagaries of love as it focuses upon the intertwined romances of several pairs of lovers. Explanatory footnotes. 80pp. 5$\frac{3}{16}$ x 8$\frac{1}{4}$. 0-486-27067-X

THE MONEY CHANGERS, Upton Sinclair. Originally published in 1908, this cautionary novel from the author of *The Jungle* explores corruption within the American system as a group of power brokers joins forces for personal gain, triggering a crash on Wall Street. 192pp. 5$\frac{3}{8}$ x 8$\frac{1}{2}$. 0-486-46917-4

THE MOST POPULAR HOMES OF THE TWENTIES, William A. Radford. With a New Introduction by Daniel D. Reiff. Based on a rare 1925 catalog, this architectural showcase features floor plans, construction details, and photos of 26 homes, plus articles on entrances, porches, garages, and more. 250 illustrations, 21 color plates. 176pp. 8$\frac{3}{8}$ x 11. 0-486-47028-8

MY 66 YEARS IN THE BIG LEAGUES, Connie Mack. With a New Introduction by Rich Westcott. A Founding Father of modern baseball, Mack holds the record for most wins — and losses — by a major league manager. Enhanced by 70 photographs, his warmhearted autobiography is populated by many legends of the game. 288pp. 5$\frac{3}{8}$ x 8$\frac{1}{2}$. 0-486-47184-5

NARRATIVE OF THE LIFE OF FREDERICK DOUGLASS, Frederick Douglass. Douglass's graphic depictions of slavery, harrowing escape to freedom, and life as a newspaper editor, eloquent orator, and impassioned abolitionist. 96pp. 5$\frac{3}{16}$ x 8$\frac{1}{4}$. 0-486-28499-9

THE NIGHTLESS CITY: Geisha and Courtesan Life in Old Tokyo, J. E. de Becker. This unsurpassed study from 100 years ago ventured into Tokyo's red-light district to survey geisha and courtesan life and offer meticulous descriptions of training, dress, social hierarchy, and erotic practices. 49 black-and-white illustrations; 2 maps. 496pp. 5$\frac{3}{8}$ x 8$\frac{1}{2}$. 0-486-45563-7

THE ODYSSEY, Homer. Excellent prose translation of ancient epic recounts adventures of the homeward-bound Odysseus. Fantastic cast of gods, giants, cannibals, sirens, other supernatural creatures — true classic of Western literature. 256pp. 5$\frac{3}{16}$ x 8$\frac{1}{4}$. 0-486-40654-7

OEDIPUS REX, Sophocles. Landmark of Western drama concerns the catastrophe that ensues when King Oedipus discovers he has inadvertently killed his father and married his mother. Masterly construction, dramatic irony. Explanatory footnotes. 64pp. 5$\frac{3}{16}$ x 8$\frac{1}{4}$. 0-486-26877-2

ONCE UPON A TIME: The Way America Was, Eric Sloane. Nostalgic text and drawings brim with gentle philosophies and descriptions of how we used to live — self-sufficiently — on the land, in homes, and among the things built by hand. 44 line illustrations. 64pp. 8$\frac{3}{8}$ x 11. 0-486-44411-2

ONE OF OURS, Willa Cather. The Pulitzer Prize–winning novel about a young Nebraskan looking for something to believe in. Alienated from his parents, rejected by his wife, he finds his destiny on the bloody battlefields of World War I. 352pp. 5³⁄₁₆ x 8¼. 0-486-45599-8

ORIGAMI YOU CAN USE: 27 Practical Projects, Rick Beech. Origami models can be more than decorative, and this unique volume shows how! The 27 practical projects include a CD case, frame, napkin ring, and dish. Easy instructions feature 400 two-color illustrations. 96pp. 8¼ x 11. 0-486-47057-1

OTHELLO, William Shakespeare. Towering tragedy tells the story of a Moorish general who earns the enmity of his ensign Iago when he passes him over for a promotion. Masterly portrait of an archvillain. Explanatory footnotes. 112pp. 5³⁄₁₆ x 8¼. 0-486-29097-2

PARADISE LOST, John Milton. Notes by John A. Himes. First published in 1667, *Paradise Lost* ranks among the greatest of English literature's epic poems. It's a sublime retelling of Adam and Eve's fall from grace and expulsion from Eden. Notes by John A. Himes. 480pp. 5³⁄₁₆ x 8¼. 0-486-44287-X

PASSING, Nella Larsen. Married to a successful physician and prominently ensconced in society, Irene Redfield leads a charmed existence — until a chance encounter with a childhood friend who has been "passing for white." 112pp. 5⅜ x 8½. 0-486-43713-2

PERSPECTIVE DRAWING FOR BEGINNERS, Len A. Doust. Doust carefully explains the roles of lines, boxes, and circles, and shows how visualizing shapes and forms can be used in accurate depictions of perspective. One of the most concise introductions available. 33 illustrations. 64pp. 5⅜ x 8½. 0-486-45149-6

PERSPECTIVE MADE EASY, Ernest R. Norling. Perspective is easy; yet, surprisingly few artists know the simple rules that make it so. Remedy that situation with this simple, step-by-step book, the first devoted entirely to the topic. 256 illustrations. 224pp. 5⅜ x 8½. 0-486-40473-0

THE PICTURE OF DORIAN GRAY, Oscar Wilde. Celebrated novel involves a handsome young Londoner who sinks into a life of depravity. His body retains perfect youth and vigor while his recent portrait reflects the ravages of his crime and sensuality. 176pp. 5³⁄₁₆ x 8¼. 0-486-27807-7

PRIDE AND PREJUDICE, Jane Austen. One of the most universally loved and admired English novels, an effervescent tale of rural romance transformed by Jane Austen's art into a witty, shrewdly observed satire of English country life. 272pp. 5³⁄₁₆ x 8¼. 0-486-28473-5

THE PRINCE, Niccolò Machiavelli. Classic, Renaissance-era guide to acquiring and maintaining political power. Today, nearly 500 years after it was written, this calculating prescription for autocratic rule continues to be much read and studied. 80pp. 5³⁄₁₆ x 8¼. 0-486-27274-5

QUICK SKETCHING, Carl Cheek. A perfect introduction to the technique of "quick sketching." Drawing upon an artist's immediate emotional responses, this is an extremely effective means of capturing the essential form and features of a subject. More than 100 black-and-white illustrations throughout. 48pp. 11 x 8¼. 0-486-46608-6

RANCH LIFE AND THE HUNTING TRAIL, Theodore Roosevelt. Illustrated by Frederic Remington. Beautifully illustrated by Remington, Roosevelt's celebration of the Old West recounts his adventures in the Dakota Badlands of the 1880s, from roundups to Indian encounters to hunting bighorn sheep. 208pp. 6¼ x 9¼. 0-486-47340-6

THE RED BADGE OF COURAGE, Stephen Crane. Amid the nightmarish chaos of a Civil War battle, a young soldier discovers courage, humility, and, perhaps, wisdom. Uncanny re-creation of actual combat. Enduring landmark of American fiction. 112pp. 5³⁄₁₆ x 8¼. 0-486-26465-3

RELATIVITY SIMPLY EXPLAINED, Martin Gardner. One of the subject's clearest, most entertaining introductions offers lucid explanations of special and general theories of relativity, gravity, and spacetime, models of the universe, and more. 100 illustrations. 224pp. 5⅜ x 8½. 0-486-29315-7

REMBRANDT DRAWINGS: 116 Masterpieces in Original Color, Rembrandt van Rijn. This deluxe hardcover edition features drawings from throughout the Dutch master's prolific career. Informative captions accompany these beautifully reproduced landscapes, biblical vignettes, figure studies, animal sketches, and portraits. 128pp. 8⅜ x 11. 0-486-46149-1

THE ROAD NOT TAKEN AND OTHER POEMS, Robert Frost. A treasury of Frost's most expressive verse. In addition to the title poem: "An Old Man's Winter Night," "In the Home Stretch," "Meeting and Passing," "Putting in the Seed," many more. All complete and unabridged. 64pp. 5³⁄₁₆ x 8¼. 0-486-27550-7

ROMEO AND JULIET, William Shakespeare. Tragic tale of star-crossed lovers, feuding families and timeless passion contains some of Shakespeare's most beautiful and lyrical love poetry. Complete, unabridged text with explanatory footnotes. 96pp. 5³⁄₁₆ x 8¼. 0-486-27557-4

SANDITON AND THE WATSONS: Austen's Unfinished Novels, Jane Austen. Two tantalizing incomplete stories revisit Austen's customary milieu of courtship and venture into new territory, amid guests at a seaside resort. Both are worth reading for pleasure and study. 112pp. 5⅜ x 8½. 0-486-45793-1

THE SCARLET LETTER, Nathaniel Hawthorne. With stark power and emotional depth, Hawthorne's masterpiece explores sin, guilt, and redemption in a story of adultery in the early days of the Massachusetts Colony. 192pp. 5³⁄₁₆ x 8¼. 0-486-28048-9

THE SEASONS OF AMERICA PAST, Eric Sloane. Seventy-five illustrations depict cider mills and presses, sleds, pumps, stump-pulling equipment, plows, and other elements of America's rural heritage. A section of old recipes and household hints adds additional color. 160pp. 8⅜ x 11. 0-486-44220-9

SELECTED CANTERBURY TALES, Geoffrey Chaucer. Delightful collection includes the General Prologue plus three of the most popular tales: "The Knight's Tale," "The Miller's Prologue and Tale," and "The Wife of Bath's Prologue and Tale." In modern English. 144pp. 5³⁄₁₆ x 8¼. 0-486-28241-4

SELECTED POEMS, Emily Dickinson. Over 100 best-known, best-loved poems by one of America's foremost poets, reprinted from authoritative early editions. No comparable edition at this price. Index of first lines. 64pp. 5³⁄₁₆ x 8¼. 0-486-26466-1

SIDDHARTHA, Hermann Hesse. Classic novel that has inspired generations of seekers. Blending Eastern mysticism and psychoanalysis, Hesse presents a strikingly original view of man and culture and the arduous process of self-discovery, reconciliation, harmony, and peace. 112pp. 5³⁄₁₆ x 8¼. 0-486-40653-9

SKETCHING OUTDOORS, Leonard Richmond. This guide offers beginners step-by-step demonstrations of how to depict clouds, trees, buildings, and other outdoor sights. Explanations of a variety of techniques include shading and constructional drawing. 48pp. 11 x 8¼. 0-486-46922-0

SMALL HOUSES OF THE FORTIES: With Illustrations and Floor Plans, Harold E. Group. 56 floor plans and elevations of houses that originally cost less than $15,000 to build. Recommended by financial institutions of the era, they range from Colonials to Cape Cods. 144pp. 8⅜ x 11. 0-486-45598-X

SOME CHINESE GHOSTS, Lafcadio Hearn. Rooted in ancient Chinese legends, these richly atmospheric supernatural tales are recounted by an expert in Oriental lore. Their originality, power, and literary charm will captivate readers of all ages. 96pp. 5⅜ x 8½. 0-486-46306-0

SONGS FOR THE OPEN ROAD: Poems of Travel and Adventure, Edited by The American Poetry & Literacy Project. More than 80 poems by 50 American and British masters celebrate real and metaphorical journeys. Poems by Whitman, Byron, Millay, Sandburg, Langston Hughes, Emily Dickinson, Robert Frost, Shelley, Tennyson, Yeats, many others. Note. 80pp. 5³⁄₁₆ x 8¼. 0-486-40646-6

SPOON RIVER ANTHOLOGY, Edgar Lee Masters. An American poetry classic, in which former citizens of a mythical midwestern town speak touchingly from the grave of the thwarted hopes and dreams of their lives. 144pp. 5³⁄₁₆ x 8¼. 0-486-27275-3

STAR LORE: Myths, Legends, and Facts, William Tyler Olcott. Captivating retellings of the origins and histories of ancient star groups include Pegasus, Ursa Major, Pleiades, signs of the zodiac, and other constellations. "Classic." — *Sky & Telescope.* 58 illustrations. 544pp. 5⅜ x 8½. 0-486-43581-4

THE STRANGE CASE OF DR. JEKYLL AND MR. HYDE, Robert Louis Stevenson. This intriguing novel, both fantasy thriller and moral allegory, depicts the struggle of two opposing personalities — one essentially good, the other evil — for the soul of one man. 64pp. 5³⁄₁₆ x 8¼. 0-486-26688-5

SURVIVAL HANDBOOK: The Official U.S. Army Guide, Department of the Army. This special edition of the Army field manual is geared toward civilians. An essential companion for campers and all lovers of the outdoors, it constitutes the most authoritative wilderness guide. 288pp. 5³⁄₁₆ x 8¼. 0-486-46184-X

A TALE OF TWO CITIES, Charles Dickens. Against the backdrop of the French Revolution, Dickens unfolds his masterpiece of drama, adventure, and romance about a man falsely accused of treason. Excitement and derring-do in the shadow of the guillotine. 304pp. 5³⁄₁₆ x 8¼. 0-486-40651-2

TEN PLAYS, Anton Chekhov. *The Sea Gull, Uncle Vanya, The Three Sisters, The Cherry Orchard,* and *Ivanov,* plus 5 one-act comedies: *The Anniversary, An Unwilling Martyr, The Wedding, The Bear,* and *The Proposal.* 336pp. 5³⁄₁₆ x 8¼. 0-486-46560-8

THE FLYING INN, G. K. Chesterton. Hilarious romp in which pub owner Humphrey Hump and friend take to the road in a donkey cart filled with rum and cheese, inveighing against Prohibition and other "oppressive forms of modernity." 320pp. 5⅜ x 8½. 0-486-41910-X

THIRTY YEARS THAT SHOOK PHYSICS: The Story of Quantum Theory, George Gamow. Lucid, accessible introduction to the influential theory of energy and matter features careful explanations of Dirac's anti-particles, Bohr's model of the atom, and much more. Numerous drawings. 1966 edition. 240pp. 5⅜ x 8½. 0-486-24895-X

TREASURE ISLAND, Robert Louis Stevenson. Classic adventure story of a perilous sea journey, a mutiny led by the infamous Long John Silver, and a lethal scramble for buried treasure — seen through the eyes of cabin boy Jim Hawkins. 160pp. 5³⁄₁₆ x 8¼. 0-486-27559-0

Browse over 9,000 books at www.doverpublications.com

THE TRIAL, Franz Kafka. Translated by David Wyllie. From its gripping first sentence onward, this novel exemplifies the term "Kafkaesque." Its darkly humorous narrative recounts a bank clerk's entrapment in a bureaucratic maze, based on an undisclosed charge. 176pp. $5\frac{3}{16}$ x $8\frac{1}{4}$. 0-486-47061-X

THE TURN OF THE SCREW, Henry James. Gripping ghost story by great novelist depicts the sinister transformation of 2 innocent children into flagrant liars and hypocrites. An elegantly told tale of unspoken horror and psychological terror. 96pp. $5\frac{3}{16}$ x $8\frac{1}{4}$. 0-486-26684-2

UP FROM SLAVERY, Booker T. Washington. Washington (1856-1915) rose to become the most influential spokesman for African-Americans of his day. In this eloquently written book, he describes events in a remarkable life that began in bondage and culminated in worldwide recognition. 160pp. $5\frac{3}{16}$ x $8\frac{1}{4}$. 0-486-28738-6

VICTORIAN HOUSE DESIGNS IN AUTHENTIC FULL COLOR: 75 Plates from the "Scientific American – Architects and Builders Edition," 1885-1894, Edited by Blanche Cirker. Exquisitely detailed, exceptionally handsome designs for an enormous variety of attractive city dwellings, spacious suburban and country homes, charming "cottages" and other structures — all accompanied by perspective views and floor plans. 80pp. $9\frac{1}{4}$ x $12\frac{1}{4}$. 0-486-29438-2

VILLETTE, Charlotte Brontë. Acclaimed by Virginia Woolf as "Brontë's finest novel," this moving psychological study features a remarkably modern heroine who abandons her native England for a new life as a schoolteacher in Belgium. 480pp. $5\frac{3}{16}$ x $8\frac{1}{4}$. 0-486-45557-2

THE VOYAGE OUT, Virginia Woolf. A moving depiction of the thrills and confusion of youth, Woolf's acclaimed first novel traces a shipboard journey to South America for a captivating exploration of a woman's growing self-awareness. 288pp. $5\frac{3}{16}$ x $8\frac{1}{4}$. 0-486-45005-8

WALDEN; OR, LIFE IN THE WOODS, Henry David Thoreau. Accounts of Thoreau's daily life on the shores of Walden Pond outside Concord, Massachusetts, are interwoven with musings on the virtues of self-reliance and individual freedom, on society, government, and other topics. 224pp. $5\frac{3}{16}$ x $8\frac{1}{4}$. 0-486-28495-6

WILD PILGRIMAGE: A Novel in Woodcuts, Lynd Ward. Through startling engravings shaded in black and red, Ward wordlessly tells the story of a man trapped in an industrial world, struggling between the grim reality around him and the fantasies his imagination creates. 112pp. $6\frac{1}{8}$ x $9\frac{1}{4}$. 0-486-46583-7

WILLY POGÁNY REDISCOVERED, Willy Pogány. Selected and Edited by Jeff A. Menges. More than 100 color and black-and-white Art Nouveau–style illustrations from fairy tales and adventure stories include scenes from Wagner's "Ring" cycle, *The Rime of the Ancient Mariner, Gulliver's Travels,* and *Faust.* 144pp. $8\frac{3}{8}$ x 11. 0-486-47046-6

WOOLLY THOUGHTS: Unlock Your Creative Genius with Modular Knitting, Pat Ashforth and Steve Plummer. Here's the revolutionary way to knit — easy, fun, and foolproof! Beginners and experienced knitters need only master a single stitch to create their own designs with patchwork squares. More than 100 illustrations. 128pp. $6\frac{1}{2}$ x $9\frac{1}{4}$. 0-486-46084-3

WUTHERING HEIGHTS, Emily Brontë. Somber tale of consuming passions and vengeance — played out amid the lonely English moors — recounts the turbulent and tempestuous love story of Cathy and Heathcliff. Poignant and compelling. 256pp. $5\frac{3}{16}$ x $8\frac{1}{4}$. 0-486-29256-8

Browse over 9,000 books at www.doverpublications.com